MIND AND RELIGION

The Ugly Reality

Edited by Schorsch Ludwig

Published 2014

ISBN-13: 978-1497590519

ISBN-10: 1497590515

www.mindandreligion.com

Table of Contents

4

Introduction

Billions of people around the world aspire to a life that offers recognition, self-esteem, love, belonging and a stress-free, prosperous life.

More than 70% of the world population turn to religion for wisdom, intelligence, compassion, morality and insight to fulfil these desires.

It is therefore perplexing that statistics show that Non-Religious people are more intelligent, compassionate, wealthy and morally robust than those seeking direction from religion.

Are these statistics just numbers categorised and averaged out? Without understanding the basic elements of religion, we must remain sceptical. We therefore provide independently verifiable data and an understanding of the relationships between Mind and Religion.

In this quest, we invite you to take a tour of thought-provoking pathways in search of new bridges for understanding Mind and Religion.

Only a trustworthy understanding can provide objectivity about Religion, Mind and Human Nature. The authors therefore sought validation of these statistical surveys from the following perspectives.

- Styles of understanding
- The evolution of religion and civilisation from the Stone Age to the 21st century
- Neuro-biology of mind, belief, intelligence, learning and the Emergence of Meaning

In all endeavours, we must understand how to succeed, but we must also understand what can fail and develop vigilance for warning signs that may lead to unpleasant surprises. That is why we also analyse aspects of the Dark Ages, Hitler's Germany, Stalin's Russia, Christian and Islamic extremism, as well as other human catastrophes.

The result is a rigorous understanding of ourselves and those who share the planet with us. This opens up new choices for developing and enriching our personal lives.

We are convinced that this understanding is of personal benefit to all readers of this treatise. Therefore, we chose to write in lay terms, free of the linguistic shortcuts found in professional jargon.

Enjoy the read!

"He (Man) must learn to understand the motives of human beings, their illusions, and their sufferings in order to acquire a proper relationship to individual fellow-men and to the community."

~Albert Einstein - Letter to The New York Times 1952

Prelude

How do we evaluate religion? Imagine four priests holding you down by your arms and legs, face up, so that you cannot escape. A fifth priest looms over you as he rips open your stomach with volcanic glass. Your anguished cry of pain is quickly stifled by the priest's fist as it thrusts through your open gut and crushes your lungs while reaching for your heart. As the pain intensifies, his hand grasps your heart and rips it out with brutal force. Still pumping, the priest raises your heart to the Sun God and thousands of shouting onlookers.... Your head is then chopped off and spiked onto a stake and displayed together with heads of other hapless victims.

Rituals like these continued for many generations in Central America before they were brutally ended by the Spanish explorer Cortes.

As a witness of these rituals, how do you respond?

Pick up weapons and decimate these tribes? Consider the morality: Is it right to kill people because you disagree with their religious rituals?

Would you rather run away before you become a sacrificial victim yourself? What about future victims left behind?

If you wish to respond to the plight of others and act in a responsible, ethical manner then do you consider peaceful, persuasive and rational influence to end such senseless, gruesome and horrific acts? But what do you know about religion, cults and human nature to be fair? What about beliefs? How can you be sure *your beliefs* are right?

Understanding

What?

My daughter was about 3 years old when we decided to go on a holiday to the coast. This was her first long trip and also her first experience of the sea.

She was very excited because we had told her so much about the sea and shown her pictures and videos. For our six or seven hour journey we had bought some music, which included the song "My Friend the Sea", which we sang until we knew all the words by heart.

Finally, when we traversed the last hill we saw a flat, misty horizon. At first it was difficult to identify what we were looking at.

"Is that it?"

"Wait" her mother said, "We will be there soon!"

As we drew closer, glimpses of the sea became more frequent, clearer and more distinguishable at every turn. We could smell the sea, then we could hear the waves and then, finally, we arrived at the sunny beach.

My daughter had become silent. There was just so much to absorb. Her hands clasped ours tightly, overwhelmed by the new experience.

When she noticed other children playing in the shallow waves, her anxiety transformed into excitement as she pulled us to the water. We could hardly keep up.

When we got to the water, carefully she put in one foot; then carefully the other. She let go of our hands and ran through the water splashing it into the air.

She stopped suddenly, quietly absorbing the extent of her experience; the rhythmic waves, the sand under her feet, the beach and the far horizon of the sea. Then the epiphany! She understood! Turning around to us, she opened her arms and shouted with joy:

"IT'S SO BIG!"

Paradigms of Understanding

"What matters is not what we think, but how we think"
~ Christopher Hitchens

A paradigm is like a map, guiding our thoughts and actions. Sometimes called perspectives, mindsets, internal representations or worldview, they are learned from the merging of experiences.

Paradigms differ for each person and each context. Understanding why we love somebody differs from the way we understand Calculus.

For example, when Galileo Galilei verified that the earth moved around the sun as understood by Copernicus, he came into direct conflict with the understanding of the universe by religion. Galileo consequently found himself under house arrest, narrowly escaping imprisonment or even burning at the stake.

On this journey, it is important that we ensure we have the right vehicle and tools for understanding sometimes difficult and obscure concepts. Subjects such as, Religion, Beliefs and Terrorism are deeply emotional issues. We cannot develop an understanding of these subjects with paradigms of abstract logic only; emotions are based on a different logic. Clinical logic or passionate rhetoric alone will not help us find solutions. We must ensure that our paradigms are unifying.

When Faith begets Doubt

Doubt begets Knowledge

Knowledge begets Understanding

Understanding begets Unity

Unity is Everything.

The Abe, Bea and Cea of Understanding

Love, Hate and Lust

We demonstrate here how different paradigms of understanding produce different outcomes. As an example, we use the paradigms of three mythical people, Abe, Bea and Cea to illustrate three different ways to understand the phenomena of "Love", "Hate" and "Lust".

Abe's Paradigms

Looking for archetypes

Abe is a "Meta" thinker. The Oxford English Dictionary defines the meta- prefix as "beyond or about" (such as meta-economics and meta-physics). Abe believes the source of understanding is a metaphysical *archetype of the phenomenon*. Understanding the *archetype* provides a model for understanding the observed phenomenon.

Abe believes emotions are part of an archetypal spirit of the soul, and therefore by understanding the soul, Abe hopes to understand emotions. Abe's paradigm is an internally referenced, theoretical and meta-physical contemplation, relying on imagination and intuition to develop understanding.

14

Bea's Paradigms
Searching for component elements

Bea is externally referenced; this understanding is based on factual observation of the properties and the *component elements of the phenomenon*. Bea considers the brain to be the main component of human behaviour and therefore examines its component elements to establish an understanding of emotions. Bea's understanding of emotions depends on a mechanistic, reductive examination of neuroscience research.

For Bea, the neuro-endocrine system is responsible for emotions, including love. It consists of a number of glands that secrete various hormones into the body, depending on specific stimuli. These hormones affect the body and prepare it for action. We experience these physical changes as emotions, feelings or moods.

The brain region responsible for regulating the neuro-endocrine system is the limbic region in the centre of the brain and includes the Thalamus, Hypothalamus, Amygdalae and Hippocampus[1]. Together they act as the circuitry of emotions and signal other parts of the brain and body to prepare for action. The limbic system also

---

[1] See appendix - The Brain

15

remembers emotionally significant events and recalls these learned responses in similar future events. [2]

Cea's Paradigms
Combining Paradigms

Cea unites Abe's meta-physical and Bea's factual observations to develop a wider understanding of emotions as a component element of a personal ecosystem. If required, Cea is prepared to expand beyond Abe's theoretical considerations or Bea's data to develop a comprehensive understanding.

> "At the heart of science is an essential balance between two seemingly contradictory attitudes — an openness to new ideas, no matter how bizarre or counterintuitive they may be, and the most ruthless skeptical scrutiny of all ideas, old and new. This is how deep truths are winnowed from deep nonsense." - ~Carl Sagan

Paradigms of Love

Abe's Love

Abe's concept of Love is that it emanates from the divine and is a manifestation of the soul, the unchanging spirit of humanity. Love must be used to develop trust and

---

[2] The Emotional Nervous System - Dr. C. George Boeree - http://webspace.ship.edu/cgboer/limbicsystem.html

fellowship and unite people. Therefore one must strive to love one's neighbour as well as one's enemies.

The love of God must be placed above all else and must be demonstrated through commitment, humility and submission.

Emotions related to Love:
Empathy, Respect, Altruism, Acceptance, Trust, Caring, Friendship and Bonding

Bea's Love

Bea's search for understanding love leads to the hormone Oxytocin.[3] It is the main hormone responsible for the feeling of love. It is produced in both men and women, although Vasopressin (in men) has an almost identical molecular structure to Oxytocin and performs similar functions. Vasopressin is also important in homeostasis, such as the regulation of water, glucose, and salts in the blood.

The presence of Oxytocin enhances the learning of social skills in early childhood and balances the immune system, thus providing protection from disease.

---

[3] A relationship between oxytocin and anxiety of romantic attachment. Donatella Marazziti et al - *Clinical Practice and Epidemiology in Mental Health* 2006

17

Its production can be stimulated by immediate or remembered experiences; for example:

- The presence of a loving person
- Touch
- Massage
- Hug
- Intimacy
- A romantic story

The physical effects of Oxytocin include:

- Relaxation of breathing and heartbeat
- Improved immune response
- Improved recognition and learning of social cues
- Stimulates child-birth

Cea's Love

Oxytocin evolved in many creatures to develop group cohesion, thus ensuring survival and development. This in turn establishes group and individual security as well as behavioural savvy carried from one generation to the next.

Romantic love is the basis of long-term relationships and parenting. Parental love is the bedrock of socially skilled children, who eventually live harmoniously within their own adult social context. Love, bonding and trust promote morally intelligent communities.[4]

Abe's list of "Emotions Related to Love" results from different *levels* of oxytocin which in turn depend on events within the personal ecology. A continuum of states of love exists from slight (trust) to intense (passionate love). For humanity to succeed, friendship and caring within the community are as important as passionate, romantic love. Building a circle of friends results in a continuum of trust and enhances ongoing affection in the home and social circle.

Love cannot be forced as it requires explicitly reciprocated behaviour within the personal ecosystem.

---

[4] The Moral Molecule - Dr. Paul J. Zak

Paradigms of Hate

Abe's Hate

Abe believes that Hate emanates from evil. It directs mankind away from the divine. Man must replace hate with love. Hate is the root cause of chaos, wars, disunity and immorality.

Emotions related to Hate

Irritation, Annoyance, Antagonism, Rage, Anger, Aggression, Loathing, Defeat, Depression, Anxiety, Panic and Fear

Bea's Hate System

For Bea, Hate is a reaction to an ongoing threat, resulting in a "Flight or Fight" response. This response is regulated by the hypothalamic-pituitary-adrenal axis (HPA or HTPA axis).[5] It is a survival mechanism and primes the body for either aggression or retreat, both of which require the same physical conditions, which are:

- Release of energy from stored sugar
- Increased heart-rate and breathing
- Tensioning of muscles for action
- Saving energy by inhibiting the immune response

---

[5] http://en.wikipedia.org/wiki/Hypothalamic-pituitary-adrenal_axis

- Saving energy by reducing rational cognitive functions
- Tunnel vision
- Constriction of certain blood vessels
- Bladder relaxation
- Pupil dilation

Adrenalin and NorAdrenalin (USA:Epinephrine and NorEpinephrine) and Cortisol are the main hormones activated by the limbic system in response to perceived threats such as:

- Physical attack
- Insult
- Aggressive behaviour
- Undermined status
- Invasion of personal space
- Ridicule
- Unmanageable workload

Threat responses are fast and immediate, beating rational contemplations by far.[6] These responses were first described by Walter Bradford Cannon in about 1914 and, depending on the type of threat stimulus, the felt emotions fall into one of two categories:

---

[6] Daniel Goleman - Emotional Intelligence –

Fight Response	Flight Response
Hate	Hate
Irritation	Loathing
Annoyance	Defeat
Antagonism	Depression
Rage	Anxiety
Anger	Panic
Wrath	Fear

Cea's Paradigm of Hate

In an untamed jungle environment, a situation of physical threat was rapidly dealt with by humans. In the city, we must often endure complex threatening situations over a length of time. In the bush the threat is soon over, either won or lost; but for city dwellers, the natural responses to threat, if not resolved, can linger for long periods of time. While the threat persists, chronic stress maintains high levels of adrenalin and cortisol which detract from the ability to think rationally and compromises the immune system.

Abe's list of "Emotions Related to Hate" can result from varying levels of stress hormones. These stress hormones create the two sets of emotions classified as either Fight or Flight response above.

Hate cannot simply be replaced by love; they are expressions of different neurological functions and serve different purposes. Believing that Hate and "bad feelings" are the work of meta-physical archetypes, such as the devil or evil, undermines our ability to solve the causes of the threat. Threats are present in the real world and therefore require real-world solutions. We usually have to change only one component element of the threat to resolve the problem.

Understanding hate and related emotions is useful; they alert us to threats. Ignoring a threat is not a good strategy, as this usually results in an escalation from hate into anxiety, fear, anger and wrath. The long-term effect of hate undermines both physical and mental health.

Paradigms of Lust and Other Sins

Abe's Lust

Abe's list of emotions relating to Lust is best articulated by Christianity's Seven Deadly Sins and by Islam's 70 major sins. According to Abe, acting on these emotions leads to eternal damnation in hell.

Christian seven deadly sins

Pride is considered the most serious of the Seven Deadly Sins and the source of the others. It is an excessive love of self, considering self more important than others and not acknowledging others.

Envy means coveting someone's status, abilities or possessions.

Greed, avarice or covetousness, is a desire for and pursuit of material possessions, a desire to acquire or possess more than one needs, especially material wealth.

Lust or lechery is a desire, usually of a sexual nature, but can also include the desire for money, fame, or power.

"Ye have heard that it was said by them of old time, Thou shalt not commit adultery: But I say unto you, That whosoever looketh on a woman to lust after her hath committed adultery with her already in his heart".

~Gospel of Matthew 5:27-28

Gluttony is over-indulgence or selfishness, placing concern with one's own interests above the well-being or interests of others.

Sloth is physical laziness, spiritual laziness, not developing spiritually, not doing the things one should do. Evil exists when good men fail to act.

Wrath: Violent rage, an uncontrolled feeling of hatred and anger. These feelings can manifest as impatience, revenge, and vigilantism.

Islamic Sins of Lust, Envy and Greed [7]

Lust: The Qur'an and the Hadith (sayings of the Prophet) prohibit lust. Lust can impinge on a person's path to Allah, as the Qur'an states, "Follow not the lusts (of your hearts), lest ye swerve (Surah 4:135)." People who act on lust are not among the believers, as the Qur'an says, "Allah doth wish to turn to you, but the wish of those who follow their lusts is that ye should turn away (from Him), far, far away (4:27)."

---

[7] See Appendix for a list of Major Sins in Islam

Pride: The disease of pride and arrogance negates all traces of goodness and piety. This is the worst vice as it causes havoc. It is a regrettable disease to have for the followers of this perfect and exalted religion. It launches a direct attack on beliefs and principles. If ignored and overlooked, it becomes fatal and incurable, and gives rise to other spiritual maladies and vices, which are no less than four in number, as mentioned below:

Envy: In Islam, envy (Hassad in Arabic) can destroy one's good deeds. Therefore, one must be content with what God has given by saying "Maashallah" (God has willed it).

Greed: "Greed is the key to trouble and carries man to hardship. It causes him to commit sin."

Bea's Lust

Testosterone is the main hormone involved in the behaviour described by Lust and other sins.[8]

Physical effects

- It determines the gender in both men and women.
- In men, it is important in developing the reproductive tissues such as the testes and

---

[8] Testosterone responses to competition predict future aggressive behaviour at a cost to reward in men – Carre' Putnam, McCormick

prostate as well as male characteristics such as bigger muscle, bone and body hair. It is also essential for health and well-being.

- In men, the concentration of testosterone is about 8 times greater than in women.
- Men consume 20 times more testosterone than women.

Behavioural effects

- Testosterone determines the sex drive in both men and women.
- Testosterone promotes status seeking, dominance and competitive behaviour.
- Higher levels of testosterone are reflected in self-confidence and risk-taking.
- High levels of testosterone are more likely to result in punitive or selfish behaviour.
- Fatherhood decreases testosterone levels in men, as paternal behaviour is triggered.

Wrath

Wrath is an extreme response to threat as described in the chapter on "Cea's Hate" above.

Sloth

Low levels of testosterone cause loss of self-esteem, defeatism and depression. There may also be other physical health problems.

Cea's Lust and other Sins

Pride, Envy, Greed, Lust, Gluttony

Testosterone is vital for the success of the human race. Every creature must compete for a place on this planet. If it fails, the creature becomes food for another. Testosterone promotes competition for status, improves self-esteem and willingness to go the extra mile.

In humans, as in most animals, competitive behaviour is abundant. From sibling rivalry to competition in business, sport, recreation and religion, we compete all the time. It is healthy to compete. As a species we thrive on competition. Great civilisations, ideas and scientific discoveries are the results of competitive behaviour.

The problems with Sin

Abe's paradigm is an example of poor solutions resulting from inadequate paradigms of understanding.

According to Pope Gregory I (540 – 604 AD), who articulated these sins, the remedy for the Seven Deadly Sins, was the threat of the wrath of God and everlasting damnation! More punitive injunctions exist in Islam.[9]

---

[9] See Appendix - Major sins according to Islam

Remedies, according to Cea

Pride: Society rewards achievers. People proudly take ownership of their achievements. It motivates both the achiever and the observer to climb greater heights of success. Success breeds success and achievements lead to greater innovation and productivity, a benefit to society at large. We should proudly declare our achievements and thereby demonstrate possibilities and challenge others to achieve the same. In this way the bar of human accomplishment is continuously raised.

Envy can be motivating, but losing a challenge can be disappointing initially. In reality the loser, by replicating the pattern of the winner, can learn how to win next time. This can be the start of greatness.

Greed is seeking the reward without entering the challenge. This behaviour can result from a lack of confidence and self-esteem when Testosterone levels are low. The remedy is to focus on preparing for the challenge rather than the reward. Preparation, proper diet and exercise help to build testosterone levels, which increases sustainable confidence and self-esteem.

Gluttony, like greed, may be the result of seeking reward and not preparing for the challenge. It can also be a biological health problem. Again, the solution is preparation for a higher goal.

Sloth or depression also results from a lack of self-esteem, pride, purpose and direction. These symptoms have a number of possible origins. There could be health issues, such as chronic fatigue, cold, influenza or any number of other health problems. These problems can usually be remedied with professional medical help. Other issues may result from the loss or separation from a loved one. "Time heals" as we know, and it can be assisted with exercise, such as walking, jogging, hiking and preparation for new achievements. This increases serotonin and testosterone, the "feel good" hormones.

Wrath, or rage, can occur when there is a perceived threat with no solution at hand or when aggressive behaviour is confronted with more aggressive responses. This increases the levels of stress hormones in both parties, escalating the situation. Breaking away from the situation and allowing the mind to click back into problem-solving mode is a remedy.

Lust, especially of a sexual nature, is one of humanity's strongest impulses and important for the success of the human race; it is driven by testosterone. During sexual activity, oxytocin is released, resulting in bonding. Oxytocin creates the attraction between people, and can lead to strong, long-lasting romantic relationships. A model of a loving, caring relationship between parents creates patterns of socially appropriate behaviour in children and adolescents.

Controlling the emotions of sexual desire is a sign of maturity and develops during the teens and the early twenties in a caring environment. Appropriate responses develop in males when women are respected and treated as equals. Women are beautiful and like to show it. Mature men express their best behaviour in the presence of intelligent and beautiful women.

Meta-physics of emotions

Assigning *metaphysical* origins to human behaviour blurs the distinction between fantasy and reality, and creates difficulties with self-control and sense of purpose. Emotions are the ultimate gauge of our personal ecology. A pragmatic paradigm for understanding emotional dynamics is a measurable way to achieving one's destiny.

Predation

Predation, as in hunting and fishing, is also driven by testosterone and an extreme form of competition. This behaviour was overlooked by Pope Gregory I, when he condemned other testosterone-driven behaviour. Predation by humans is an evolutionary remnant of our primate origins and is therefore difficult to grasp by Creationists. Predation, even in recent history, was difficult to understand by organised religion and remained unchecked in its corridors before it became a secular criminal matter.

> "People may choose to ignore their animal heritage by interpreting their behavior as divinely inspired, socially purposeful, or even self-serving, all of which they attribute to being human, but they masticate, fornicate, and procreate, much as chimps and apes do, so they should have little cause to get upset if they learn that they act like other primates when they politically agitate, debate, abdicate, placate, and administrate, too."
>
> ~ Arnold M. Ludwig - King of the Mountain: The Nature of Political Leadership (2002)

Captain of the Cea

Cea's brain

Emotions play a critical role in our lives. Without them we would not respond to threats or needs of any kind. We would fail to bond socially and lack preferences. We would be like toys without batteries, still parked where we were born, devoid of motivation.

We have learned, in a summarised fashion, about elements of the mind and how emotions shape our character, health, perceptions, reasoning, morality, beliefs and destiny.

To be captain of one's destiny requires uniting the dream, imagination and fantasy of Abe with down-to-earth data from Bea. Only then can we prepare for the tasks ahead.[10]

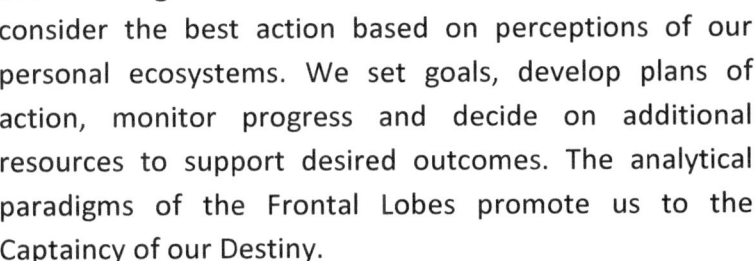

How do we captain our destiny? Just inside the forehead is the executive region of the brain, which at the age of 25, is the last part of the brain to mature. We use this region of the brain to consider the best action based on perceptions of our personal ecosystems. We set goals, develop plans of action, monitor progress and decide on additional resources to support desired outcomes. The analytical paradigms of the Frontal Lobes promote us to the Captaincy of our Destiny.

The brain rewards these functions with dopamine-sensitive neurons. Dopamine is a pervasive neuro-transmitter that produces "feels right" epiphanies.

---

[10] Neuropsychiatry, Neuropsychology, Clinical Neuroscience – Rhawn Joseph, Ph.D

It is useful to remember that the Frontal Lobes must be developed through use. ***Use it or lose it!*** The more active the brain, the easier and more accomplished our solutions become.

Mind and Reality

Understanding how the mind perceives reality from sensory input is prerequisite for understanding responses to the external world, i.e. behaviour.

Perceptions of the external world are biased representations of reality, as explained in the following paragraphs. How then can one ensure reliable perceptions that generate appropriate responses? This is the subject of this chapter.

Beliefs and Tolerance

We have beliefs for every occasion: work, school, education, politics, self, neighbours, poverty, wealth, health and religion. We start accumulating beliefs from the day we were born. Experiences embed themselves into our memories and influence perceptions of new experiences. Therefore, early experiences bias later perceptions and behaviour. This bias of perceptions we call beliefs. The assimilation of a mosaic of beliefs determines behaviour patterns, personality, values and morality. They determine the life we lead.

Why we believe

> "I know of no society in human history that ever suffered because its people became too desirous of evidence in support of their core beliefs."

36

~ Sam Harris - Letter to a Christian Nation

Beliefs are an important element of the learning system and use personal experience as data. Every moment of the day, we are bombarded with data from our senses. Beliefs use previous experience to speed up the decisions we have to make. This is how we learn to walk, talk, and run. This works out fine, if the beliefs are appropriate for the prevailing situation.

Beliefs do not need any proof, only limited experience. When experiences are not representative of the real world, beliefs will be disjoint from the real world.

Beliefs have considerable influence on the life's journey. For example, beliefs about self, influenced by early childhood experiences, will reflect in the choices we make in adult life.

 To better understand how beliefs evolve, we must first understand more about the functionalities of the brain.

Almost all areas of the brain are involved in integrating information from the senses to develop appropriate responses. The human brain consists of a large matrix of neurons that communicate with each other by transmitting tiny bursts of electric energy. On the input side of the neuron, a number of dendrites receive electric impulses from preceding neurons. Depending on the pattern of these input signals, the neuron will trigger its own electric impulse through the axons to the dendrites of the following neurons.[11]

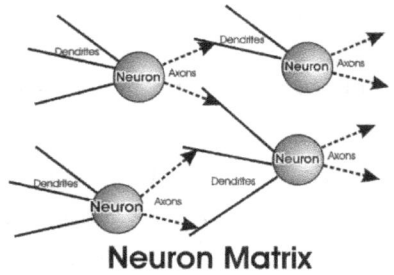

Neuron Matrix

The patterns received by a neuron through its dendrites are key. These patterns act like passwords; only the correct pattern will trigger its neuron to pass on the electric pulse through the axons to the dendrites of the next neuron. After a series of successive levels of the process, the brain gradually produces an inner representation of the sensed world in the conscious mind.

If the same patterns are triggered regularly, then the connections in those pathways are strengthened, thus creating memory. If the senses repeatedly feed biased data then biased memory will be strengthened, resulting in biased beliefs, which lead to biased thoughts, decisions and behaviour.

---

[11] Mammalian Brain – Barry W. Conners and Michael A. Long – Neuroscience Journal

"... two cells or systems of cells that are repeatedly active at the same time will tend to become 'associated', so that activity in one facilitates activity in the other." ~Donald Hebb 1949.

The brain activity is enormous. One neuron can have thousands of dendrites and axons. There are about 100 billion neurons in the brain, creating a network of trillions of connections.

ANN - Artificial Neural Networks

Artificial intelligence experts have increased the understanding of neuron functionality by modelling the neural functions on computers. These models are now also used in practical applications, such as recognition of faces, voices and language. These systems are also used in cameras, language translation, sales predictions and crime detection.

Let's face it

Reality

Here is a very basic example of face recognition processes to assist us to understand the formation of thoughts and beliefs. A computer, programmed with an Artificial Neural Network (ANN)

39

algorithm, is instructed to find a face in this image from the pixels taken by a modern camera.

Patterns of pixels with similar properties, such as brightness and dimensions, are identified by ANN. Similar patterns, such as the circles, ellipses and triangles, are stored with their physical dimensions and relationships to each other.

Belief

This image, produced by ANN, is an early attempt to find the face. There are, as we can see, some features that are not realistic. How should ANN know where features begin and end? Also, how does the ANN decide if incidental shadings are facial features? How does the ANN know which is a genuine feature and which is not? For this, ANN uses sophisticated mathematical approximation methods. In humans, the *fusiform face area* of the brain, near the occipital lobe at the back of the head, processes images in very similar ways. [12]

---

[12] *Robot Vision* - Horn, Berthold K.P.

Tolerance and Reality

Biased beliefs are the result of biased information. To get closer to reality, we must be open to more information. As you can see, ANN believes that the dark patch over the left eye is a feature of a human face! This is a tentative belief, like Palaeolithic man believing that gods make thunder. The ability of ANN to adjust its image to reality depends on its tolerance level. The _intolerant_ ANN will reject new images of faces without the shading as "*not a face!*" Fortunately, the tolerance level in a computer is a parameter which can be changed easily.

Change to more realistic beliefs requires more data, tolerance, discrimination and analytical processing.

Intelligence

Before the 1960's many scientists believed that the number of neurons in the brain was constant and the brain did not develop. It was believed that the brain we were born with is the same brain that we die with. That belief changed when more data became available.

Neuroscience research now reveals that the number of brain cells and their inter-connections grow continuously as we exercise the brain. Learning creates new neural interconnections and strengthen old ones. For example, from birth to the age of five, the brain mass of a child

41

doubles to accommodate the huge learning requirements for both physical and cognitive skills.

"Neuro-plasticity" describes the performance improvement that is gained by the development of neural connections each time a signal passes through a neuron, making it more efficient. This is the foundation of learning. It results in good memory, habit, professional insight, intuition, beliefs and intelligence.

Neuro-plasticity is equivalent to building muscles with strenuous physical workouts. With the right nutrition and the right kind of mental exercising, the growth of "brain-muscles" helps us understand more complex issues.

Observe how successful people exercise their brains intensely!

Altered States

We all love a good story about super heroes. But to really enjoy stories of fiction, we must disengage from reality. This is one example of an Altered State.

"Altered state of consciousness" is a term first used in 1966 by Arnold M. Ludwig and refers to a reduced external awareness. Methods of inducing altered states involve focusing on the inner experience by reducing external sensory perception. An Altered State occurs spontaneously during periods of sensory deprivation, lack of sleep, isolation, fever, fasting, oxygen-deprivation, decompression sickness, trauma, dancing, aesthetic experience or temporal lobe epilepsy. During altered states, activities in some areas of the Frontal Lobes (responsible for monitoring and controlling thoughts) are inhibited, similar to falling asleep, resulting in reduced critical reasoning.

Often described as 'transcendence' or 'trance', these mental states can be induced deliberately in many ways; including hypnosis, meditation, prayer, lucid dreaming, aesthetic appreciation, activities such as yoga and various forms of dance.

Forms of Altered States

Hypnosis

This is arguably the best-known form of deliberately inducing an altered state of consciousness, usually by a trained hypnotist. After hypnotic induction, the subject is persuaded to blur the gap between reality and imagination. Once inner awareness is enhanced, imagined scenarios take on a sense of reality. Skilled therapists can use this state to facilitate modification of internal representation and change self-defeating beliefs.

Meditation

The variety of meditation techniques, including all forms of rituals and prayer, are endless. The experiences are usually interpreted to match the expectation; such as "Receiving clear vision", "Out-of-body experience", "Communicating with god", "Receiving eternal wisdom" "Feeling a presence", "Being touched by angels" or "Communicating with the ancestors".

A personal experience
During the early 1980's, like so many others, I had learned a meditation technique and decided to spend a weekend in the mountains with other initiates and teachers. After days of yoga, vegetarian food, meditations and easy conversation, the meditations reached a natural flow.

As I drifted into a trance, the mantra became very gentle and quiet until it disappeared, as did my thoughts. In this stillness there was a feeling of peace and timelessness which resulted in a sense of unity with the cosmos. Everything felt perfect in this intense, overwhelming sense of bliss. In this state the only apparent reality, I noticed, was the internal experience, disconnected from all else.

I later approached one of the teachers and related my experience to him. He listened carefully until I had finished. He put his hand on my shoulder and said: "That is a wonderful example of God consciousness". "Wow!" I thought "I wonder how many atheists have God consciousness".

Peak Experiences

This is another form of Altered States. It is an intense epiphany and can be triggered by aesthetic beauty in art, music or understanding.

"To summarize, it looks quite probable that the peak experience may be the model of the religious revelation or the religious illumination or conversion which has played so great a role in the history of religions. But, because peak-experiences are in the natural world and because we can research with them and investigate them, and because our knowledge of such experiences is growing and may be confidently expected to grow in the future, we may now fairly hope to understand more about the big revelations, conversions, and illuminations upon which the high religions were founded."

- Abraham Maslow - "Religions, Values, and Peak Experiences"

Searching for the Soul

In religion, altered state experiences are often interpreted as experiences of the soul or spirit communicating with the Divine and are therefore of special interest. A number of people have attempted to articulate an understanding.

St Thomas Aquinas

"..in each body the whole soul is in the whole body and whole in each part of it"..."The soul is in every part of the body just as whiteness is in each part of a blank sheet of paper, although some organs, such as the heart, can have a special significance."

~St Thomas Aquinas - *On the Trinity*, book 6

Ibn Sina - Islam

Asserts that we infer the existence of the soul because we observe bodies that perform certain acts with some degree of will, such as eating, growing, reproducing, moving and perceiving. Bodies do not have will, therefore these acts must belong to a principle other than bodies. This principle is what is called 'soul'.

René Descartes

This French Renaissance Philosopher, known mainly for the phrase "I think therefore I am", believed that the pineal gland was the seat of the soul. This because he found it to be the only component of the brain that exists as a single entity rather than two halves, "thereby connecting the intellect with the body".

Modern neuro-scientists, now understand the function of the pineal gland to be responsible for the production of melatonin, which helps to regulate the sleep-wake cycle by causing drowsiness. It is stimulated by darkness.

Michael Persinger

Is a cognitive neuroscience researcher who proposed that mystical experiences can be explained by changes in the temporal lobe of the brain.

The "Koren helmet" (named after its inventor Stanley Koren) was used by Michael Persinger to study creativity and the effects of subtle stimulation of the temporal lobes with low-intensity magnetic pulses. While wearing this helmet, many subjects reported "mystical experiences and altered states".

Andrew Newberg

A neuroscientist and author of a number of publications on neuro-theology proposes, that mystical experiences involve changes in the prefrontal cortex and parietal lobe, in addition to changes in the limbic system and parts of the temporal lobe.[13]

Revelations and Mystical Experiences

Many studies of altered states of consciousness in Neuro-Science show that Revelations and Mystical Experiences are phenomena resulting from hyperactivity in the right temporal lobe of the brain. Hallucinations, fantasies, imagination, dreaming, daydreaming, hypnotic suggestibility and a variety of creative activities are also produced in this brain region. [14]

The Existence of God

Before we can reach any conclusions about the meaning of Revelations and Mystical Experiences, we must first eliminate the possibility of:-

- Post- or pre-hypnotic suggestions
- Placebo effect
- Dreaming or daydreaming
- Fantasy
- Health issues
- Environmental factors such as sensory deprivation and fasting.

---

[13] Principles of Neurotheology

[14] Evolution and the Neuroanatomy of Religious Experience - Rhawn Joseph

"Revelations" and "Mystical Experiences" do not equate to organised Religion. Interpretations of these experiences as a communion with some God, do not define a religion. Even atheists, who do not involve god, experience "Mystic Revelations".

The Evolution of Religion

Everything happens within the context of an ecology. Our interest is the study of the *dynamics* of human ecologies that influenced events in the evolution of religion. To understand Religion today, we should also be aware of the elements that shaped it through history. The needs and pressures on humanity in history have produced a humanity we live in today. To understand religious activity today, we must understand its evolution.

Prehistoric Religion

Every creature is dependant for its survival on its ecology. Fish will perish out of water and birds perish in water.

The one-sided dependence on nature's ecosystems by humans, changed about 300 000 years ago, when they took control of fire. [15] They could then protect themselves from insects and predators at night and cook food to produce a more varied diet.

To gain control of an ecosystem necessitates understanding it first. In previous chapters we have demonstrated the requirements for a practical, workable understanding. Early humans lacked the paradigms for

---

[15] Hominid Use of Fire in the Lower and Middle Pleistocene. Steven R James.

understanding ecosystems that are more complex. In an attempt to reach out for understanding, they turned to supernatural explanations. Beliefs in deities and spirits filled tantalising gaps in knowledge that could not be filled in any other way.

The earliest evidence of religious behaviour in humans is the ritual burials of their deceased, indicating a belief in the afterlife. The transition from ancestor worship to belief in superhuman deities was inevitable. In order to influence their ecology they coaxed deities with supplications, sacrifices and rituals. Whatever worked once, as a random event, was accepted as the gods' preference. These beliefs were ritualised and integrated into the religion and culture of the tribe.

The Human Predator

Early man had to hunt for his food; killing and slaughtering was a part of life. Mayan and Aztec human sacrifice rituals may have been ritualized predatory behaviour and so also the biblical Abraham's intended sacrifice of his son.

The predator instinct is still present today, displaying its fearsome teeth when the situation arises. Computer games, business language, sport and other entertainments indicate how humanity has learned to manage the impulse.

Evolution of Villages

When humans took greater control of their ecosystems by domesticating animals and growing food from seeds, the need to migrate to fresh natural resources was reduced. They began to settle down and build permanent structures to provide safety, comfort, protection from the elements and food storage for off-season needs.

In tribal camps everyone knew everybody. When these camps developed into villages, tasks could be divided and became more specialised. Some baked bread, while others made shoes and so on. A uniform, measurable value of the diverse tasks created a need for a standard value currency and the beginning of a commercial system. This required the development of more sophisticated arithmetic and mathematical skills. Calculation of architectural relationships, weight and volume, time and distance became important, as villages also became trading destinations. These developments helped to develop the brain for a better understanding of ecosystems.

Living in one geographic location brought on new dangers. Marauding groups could loot the resources painstakingly acquired. A form of militia was now required, which could protect the village and reciprocate the looting behaviour.

New Leadership Styles Emerge

As villages grew, leaders took on new roles. Personal contact between the leaders and citizens became less frequent. Indeed, leaders began to isolate themselves and delegate administrative tasks to others. Tribal leaders became kings, levied taxes for administration, which included their own expenses. The ruling class surrounded itself with an aura of deity, enhancing the justification of their leadership and payment of taxes.

As civilisations developed so also religions developed. Prehistoric villages show evidence of temples and places of worship. Stone carvings indicate the variety of gods worshiped. Religion was a major facet of everyone's life, actively encouraged by the elite. No important decisions were made without referring to the gods. Merging the code of conduct of society with the authority of the gods became a persuasive tool for the elite to control the behaviour of citizens.

Ancient Greece

Ancient Greek philosophy is an indication of the mental landscape of early civilised societies. These philosophies formed the foundation for the theology of the major religions of today, especially, Judaism, Christianity and Islam.

Athens was typical of a village that developed into a small city and thus posed particular challenges for the ruling elite. Practical problems, such as water reticulation, waste disposal and town planning required new procedures, codes of conduct and systems of governance. This required paradigms that were more sophisticated. This reflects in the change in religions.

Early Greek religion typified the polytheistic cultures of the time. Their mythology was extensive, comprising over 60 deities, creatures and places. Deities were believed to live in a mystical realm and together controlled all the natural phenomena as well as personal desires, traits and destiny. Religious rituals were an important part of everyday life. Great expenditure and effort went into building temples and effigies of deities.

The mythology surrounding the Greek gods was an attempt to explain every aspect of human existence, including the origin of the world and the afterlife.

Together they created confusing and bizarre scenarios. Here is an example:

> "Prometheus created the shape of all earthly creatures out of mud while Athena breathed life into them. Epimetheus gave creatures qualities such as cunning, strength, wings and fur. Unfortunately Epimetheus ran out of qualities when it came to mankind so Prometheus gave mankind the ability to stand upright like the gods."

To make better sense of it all, two paradigms of philosophy evolved: pragmatic paradigms and meta-physical orientated paradigms.

Pragmatic Philosophers

Aristotle (384 BC – 322 BC).

Aristotle (384 BC – 322 BC), was a student of Plato and a teacher to Alexander the Great. His expertise covered virtually the entire knowledge base of the ancient world such as physics, metaphysics, the arts, philosophy, politics, governance, ethics, biology, and zoology. Together with Plato and Socrates, Aristotle is considered one of the founders of Western philosophy.

Aristotle created a comprehensive system of formal logic, underpinning Western philosophical debate even today.

"Spoken words are symbols or signs of affections or impressions of the soul; written words are the signs of words spoken."
Aristotle - *On Interpretation*

Archimedes (287 BC –212 BC)

Archimedes is known for his innovative contributions to mathematics, physics, engineering and astronomy. He is regarded as one of the leading scientists and mathematicians in classical antiquity. Among his advances in physics are the foundations of hydrostatics, statistics and an explanation of the principle of the lever. He is credited with inventing machines such as siege engines and the screw pump that bears his name. Modern experiments have successfully verified claims of Archimedes' machine designs that were capable of lifting attacking ships out of the water and setting them on fire by focusing an array of mirrors on them.

Archimedes Screw

This invention transfers water from a low-lying body of water into irrigation canals. Engineers still use this principle today for pumping liquids and granulated solids.

The principles of Levers

Archimedes discovered the magnification of force with the use of levers. "Give me a place to stand on, and I will move the Earth." He also designed a "block and tackle" system to lift heavy loads.

A precursor to Integral Calculus

Using a "method by exhaustion", Archimedes was able to calculate the area enclosed by a parabola and a straight line. He also discovered the method of calculating the area and radius of a circle. These methods were later advanced by Isaac Newton into what is now known as Calculus.

Specific Gravity

To determine the quality of gold in King Hiero II's crown, Archimedes needed to determine the volume of the irregular shaped crown to determine its specific gravity so as to compare it with the specific gravity of genuine gold. He could easily determine the weight of the crown, but calculating the volume was a problem. By observing that the water level rose when he got into his bath, he concluded that a body immersed in a fluid displaces the same volume of the fluid as the immersed body. Thus he solved the problem of the quality of gold in the King's crown. This gave rise to the legend of Archimedes running through the streets dressed in nothing more than an epiphany shouting "Eureka! Eureka" (I've got it! I've got it!)

Metaphysical Philosophers

The following philosophers were meta-physical thinkers, looking for answers by introspection.

Socrates (469 – 399 BC)

Socrates was suspicious of sensory observations. "If you put a straight stick halfway in the water, it will look bent. Take it out and it looks straight again. Is the stick really straight or are our senses trying to trick us?" Therefore, by anecdotal example, he concludes that the senses are unreliable and thus introspection is the only reliable path to truth.

When Socrates asserted, "the senses cannot be trusted" he disconnected himself from the sensed world, possibly creating a permanent altered state.

> "The greatest blessing granted to mankind come by way of madness, which is a divine gift." — Socrates

Socrates explains the process of enlightenment in the following, now famous, Allegory. This and other allegories are found in the "Republic" by Plato, who kept note of Socrates' interactions with students.[16]

A paraphrase of the Allegory of the Cave

"Imagine a group of people who have lived chained in a cave all of their lives. These people watch shadows projected from behind them onto a wall with the use of fire. The prisoners can only see these shadows. According to Socrates (as described by Plato), the shadows are closest to reality as the prisoners will get. He then explains that a philosopher is like a prisoner who has been freed from the cave and comes to understand that the shadows on the wall do not make up reality. The philosopher perceives the hidden forms rather than the mere shadows seen by other prisoners. The prisoners however perceive only shadows of these unseen objects (Forms)." [17]

Plato (428 BC – 348 BC)

In the following paragraphs, the novice reader of this philosophy should not be concerned about understanding the unusual nature of Plato's forms. We must be aware that this was an Ancient Greek philosopher's paradigm for trying to understand phenomena without verifiable factual evidence.

---

[16] Plato's Republic – Alan Jacobs
[17] Allegory of the Cave-Plato's Republic – Book VII Alan Jacobs

Plato extends Socrates' philosophy by elaborating on the concept of Forms as a way of understanding how internal representations, such as ideas, arise.

Plato believed that there exists an ideal, mystical state from where these "Forms" are instantiated. For him knowledge and intelligence are the abilities to grasp this mystical world of Forms with one's mind. All perceived objects are an instance of some generic archetype of the object, which exists in this ideal metaphysical state. These archetypes he refers to as Forms. Archetypes include observed properties such as colours and shapes but also human attributes such as wisdom and courage.

To explain how archetypes transform from the ideal state to the real world, Plato believed that an *artisan-type entity* is responsible for instantiating and maintaining objects and their properties in the physical universe. This artisan entity was called the "Demiurge", from the Greek word meaning "public worker".

Through the words of Socrates, Plato describes in "Republic" how the world was created by "the Good" according to the patterns of the idealistic Forms. Man's proper service to "the Good" is cooperation in the implementation of the ideal, from the world of archetypes; that is, in miming the Good.

To this end Plato described details of the proper imitation of "the Good"; however Justice, Beauty, Courage, Temperance, Wisdom and others, cannot be known. But, according to Plato, they can be known to some degree through the instantiated copies, with great difficulty and to varying degrees by some people.

Plotinus (204 – 270 AD) [18]

Some 500 years after Socrates and Plato, in his work "Enneads", the philosopher Plotinus gave "the Good" a personality. Thus he and his teacher, Ammonius Saccas, transformed Plato's philosophy of an ideal space of the Good into the Divine.

Plotinus believed that there is a supreme, transcendent "One", containing no division, multiplicity or distinction. It was beyond all Forms. The "One" cannot be like anything that exists, nor is it the unity of all things. It existed prior to anything else.

For Plotinus, the contemplative part of human beings is the soul, which is superior to all material things. The soul is pre-existent, and immortal. According to Plotinus, real human happiness is not dependent on the physical world,

---

[18] http://plato.stanford.edu/entries/plotinus/

but is dependent on the metaphysical world as found in the highest capacity of reason. (A type of altered state)

Neo-platonism

Other philosophers who elaborated on Plato's philosophy, include Plutarch, the Neopythagoreans, and Numenius of Apamealater. The elaborated versions later became known as Neo-Platonism and influenced Christian theologians such as St Augustine of Hippo and Islamic theologians, such as Abu Yusuf ibn Ishaq al-Kindi.

St Augustine described mystical contemplation as a means to encounter God or "the One" directly, reporting at least two mystical experiences in his confessions.

The Greco-Roman Period

Ancient political boundaries were fluid. Anyone could, with sufficient military force, raid neighbouring civilisations, pillage their assets and then divert tax revenue from the subjugated population into their own coffers.

Alexander the Great (356 – 323 BC), a pupil of Aristotle, extended the Greek empire through the Middle East and North Africa into what is now Macedonia, Turkey, Egypt, Armenia, Syria, Persia as far as the Himalayan mountains and the borders of India.

In 146 BC the Greek empire succumbed to superior Roman military forces at Corinth and signalled the beginning of the Greco-Roman period.

The merged Roman Empire was huge, covering almost all of Europe including parts of the British Isles, central Asia, Egypt and Persia. All languages, cultures, religions, rituals, rites and beliefs that fell within this empire became part of a melting pot of a large number of myths, fables, gods, demi-gods, angels, demons, dogmas, rituals and festivals. Cities, towns and villages had their own patron deity. Households espoused favoured deities; the front door and back door could have different spiritual guardians.

By choosing and worshiping favoured gods, it was hoped that life improvements and support would be forthcoming from these gods. A soldier worshiped a war-god; a suitor for the object of affection would worship the love-god, hoping to improve the chances of success. Pleasing the gods with rituals and offerings would, hopefully, bring about desired results. However, the heavenly domains often contradicted each other, causing confusion.

Despite the diversity of religions, there was, for the most part, a mutual respect for different faiths. People showed tolerance of different religious viewpoints. It seems that people took an eclectic approach to their religion and respected the choices of others.

Monotheism: The Beginning

With so many religious options, a complex spiritual world existed. Each deity had its own rules of conduct, rituals and ethos. Fortunately, monotheistic religions such as Judaism, Zoroastrianism and Manicheism provided an example of simpler religions with the added opportunity to enhance the status of the ruling elite by claiming ownership of the combined power of all gods.

Advantages of Monotheistic Religions

Wars were ugly and brutal, involving face-to-face battles, resulting in slow death from infections, serious injury and rivers of blood. The Emperor and his Generals needed strong motivational leverage. A perception of the Emperor as a descendant of a God with supernatural powers was a very useful ingredient. Once this was accepted, monotheistic religions were readily accepted.

A pervasive belief in the divine guidance of the ruling elite had existed since the beginning of religion. Egyptian and Roman leaders in particular claimed to be direct descendants of the gods. "The Son of God" title existed at least from the earliest pharaohs. In monotheistic religions, leaders compared themselves to the one single all-powerful God who embodied traits such as courage, wisdom, leadership and judgement.

Common citizens easily accepted the monotheistic God because it also personified caring in a relationship with the individual, conceived as a caring father figure who is all-powerful, all-seeing and all-knowing and therefore more powerful than any single polytheistic god.

The time was ripe for a religion that went beyond an explanation of natural phenomena, and addressed issues concerning everyday personal experiences of citizens, such as relationships and self-realization.

Early Monotheist Religions

Egyptian Monotheism

"The formal religious practice centered on the pharaoh, the king of Egypt. Although he was human, the pharaoh was believed to be descendant from the gods, and was obliged to sustain the gods through rituals and offerings so that they could maintain the universe. Therefore, the state dedicated enormous resources to the performance of these rituals and to the construction of the temples where they were carried out. Individuals could also interact with the gods for their own purposes."

– Jan Assman – Egyptologist - "Death and Salvation in Ancient Egypt"

Egyptian monotheism is arguably the first of its kind to reflect an example of organised monotheistic religions preceding Christianity.

Akhenaten (died around 1336 BC), changed his name from Amenhotep (IV) in the fifth or sixth year after ascendance to power. He ordered the construction of a new capital city, Akhetaten ("Horizon of Aten") near modern Armarna and vowed never again to leave the city. Four years later he declared that Aten was the only god, and that he was the only intermediary between Aten and the people.

By establishing this new order and rejecting previous gods in favour of the Aten, he took religion away from the influential priests. Citizens were only permitted to worship Aten through the pharaoh and the royal family. This new religion gave the pharaoh absolute power over secular and religious life in Egypt.

Akhenaten ruled for 17 years before he died, having established one of the earliest institutional monotheistic religions. Many scholars consider him, as having pioneered monotheism. However, after his death traditional Egyptian polytheistic religion was reinstated by his successor, stranding those who had converted to Akhenaten's monotheism.

This is likely a basis of the biblical exodus from Egypt into Judea and the formation of Israel. An early reference to Israel is found on the Merneptah Stele (a commemorative obelisk), also known as the Israel Stele, which shows an inscription by the Egyptian king Merneptah (reigned: 1213 - 1203 BC), mentioning Isrir (Israel). This Stele also helps to validate the timeline of the exodus.

> "Moses believed in Akhenaten's God Aten. After Akhenaten's death and the return to polytheism in Egypt, Moses was forced to leave with his fellow monotheists."
> ~Sigmund Freud - "Moses and Monotheism"

Zoroastrianism pre-existed Christianity in the southern Arabian Peninsula and was based on the teachings of Prophet Zoroaster (Zarathustra). At its peak it was one of the world's largest religions. It was founded some time before 500 BC in Greater Iran. According to the teachings of Zoroaster, the Creator, Ahura Mazda, is all good. Ahirman, the evil, will attempt to destroy creation. Followers must combat evil by obeying Zoroastrian teachings which define Ahura Mazda as the supreme God of all other gods of other religions.

Zoroastrians taught that on dying, everyone must cross the Bridge of Judgment. Their actions under free will determine the outcome. One is either greeted at the bridge by a beautiful maiden or by an ugly, smelly old woman. The maiden leads the dead across the bridge to the Amesha Spenta (Good Mind), who carries them to paradise. The old woman leads the dead down a bridge that narrows until they fall into the abyss of hell.

The Origin of Christianity

Judea

King David started building a permanent temple in Jerusalem. His son Solomon finally completed it.

During the period leading up to the first century BC, Rome had deliberately and steadily undermined the Jewish culture and religion by its occupation of Judea in an attempt to subjugate the Jews.

The Roman governor of Judea, Herod "The Great" (73BC – 4BC) had rebuilt and expanded the Temple of Solomon, previously destroyed by the Babylonians, and subsequently took control of the hiring and firing of priests. Herod was named "King of the Jews" by Rome, as was the custom for governors of conquered territories. His descendant, Agrippa II, inherited this title in 48 AD. Agrippa continued with the appointment and deposal of Jewish high priests, ensuring their allegiance to Rome and subjugation of the Jewish people. The discontent of the Jews came to a head in 66 AD when Greeks performed pagan rituals at the Jewish temple. Tolerated by the Greek-speaking soldiers, this was highly offensive to the Jews. Jewish citizens of Jerusalem then forced the soldiers out of Jerusalem. Agrippa II responded by putting the city under siege in early 70AD.

The suffering of the Jews besieged in Jerusalem was immense as starvation and illness set in. Some Jews managed to escape through tunnels, but if caught were crucified and displayed to the city from the hills surrounding Jerusalem. After months, the Roman soldiers broke through and massacred or enslaved the remaining emaciated men, women and children.

During and after the siege, a story about a great saviour was irresistibly compelling. Based on their immediate experience, the story of crucifixions, feeding of the starved, cleansing of the temple, martyrdom and resurrection became strongly fixated into the minds of survivors.

Jews who had escaped or been captured and enslaved, spread this very compelling story around the Mediterranean and wherever they found themselves. The story of Jesus, as a living person, who was the embodiment of God, walking among the people and suffering and dying on their behalf and then resurrected to go to heaven, was very appealing, especially to people suffering hardship.

Roman Empire Crumbling

Even as Jerusalem fell, the cost of maintaining security in the large empire became exceedingly burdensome to the

Roman Empire. The challenge of administering a geographic area which, today constitutes over 30 countries, reaching as far as Western Europe, Asia Minor and North Africa, exhausted enormous resources in organization, money and militia. Security issues, resulting from sporadic invasion by tribes from the north and east, required continuous training and deployment of militia. The expense of governing the Empire was more than Rome could muster. Gold coins were diluted with non-precious metals. This devaluation created hyperinflation. The militia was reduced in size. Travel became risky, and trade collapsed, creating an economic depression. Internal dissent and conflicts disrupted the Roman Empire as generals competed for pieces of the Empire. Price control policies, installed by Diocletian, further disrupted the flow of the economy. Citizens suffered severe shortages as well as an insecure personal environment. Depressed and impoverished, the populace began to question the divinity of their emperor, Diocletian. [19]

Diocletian

Diocletian turned to his pagan priests to obtain re-assurance from the gods. After reading the entrails of sacred animals, the priests returned with bad news. Even

---

[19] Edward Gibbon, *The Decline and Fall of the Roman Empire*

the Oracle of Delphi was negative. Diocletian's advisors blamed monotheistic religions for the non-compliant entrails and Diocletian began persecuting monotheistic religions.

Manichaeism

Manichaeism, a major Gnostic religion (based on the ideas of Plotinus), was bigger in membership than Christianity. Its influence extended from China in the east to the Hispanic Peninsula in the west. Its prophet Mani (216–276 AD) described the universe as a conflict between the spiritual world of light and the material world of darkness and the human person as the battleground of these powers. Manicheans believed in the existence of evil as Satan's war against God. Manicheans believed Jesus to have three separate identities; Jesus the Luminous, Jesus the Messiah and Jesus the Sufferer.

Manicheans were mercilessly persecuted by Diocletian. They were either killed or enslaved. Leaders were burnt alive. To escape persecution, many Manicheans converted to Christianity.

Diocletian then turned against the Christians. Many Christians escaped with the help of sympathetic Pagans. Martyrdom injunctions strengthened the resolve of the surviving Christians who resisted changing their religious conviction.

Galerius

When the massacre of many Christians saw no end to Christianity, the exhausted Diocletian retired. Galerius succeeded Diocletian as Emperor and ended the persecution of Christians with the Edict of Toleration in 311AD, signed by Galerius, Constantine and Licinius (Emperors of the three major regions of the Roman Empire).

Constantine

Constantine had won the imperial crown in 306 AD after a short war. Factionalism in the empire was rife. Even different Christian sects were fighting each other. Constantine needed a way to unify the Empire and inspire his people against the invading tribes. Unifying the Christian factions would increase his support base and bring an end to expensive persecutions. The Edict of Milan restored Christian property in 313 AD, signed by the Emperors, Constantine of the West and Licinius of the East.

First Council of Nicaea

In 325 AD Constantine convened the First Council of Nicaea (present-day Iznik in Turkey). The purpose of the

Council was to resolve disagreements about Christian doctrine and to unify Christians, but it also placed Constantine in firm control of all religions, including the assembly representing Christians.

Jews who had converted to Christianity and who had escaped or were captured during the fall of Jerusalem were dispersed in various regions around the Mediterranean Sea. There each group propagated their own version of Christianity. The number of different gospels that emerged reflects this. Constantine set himself the task of consolidating the theology of Christianity into one unified Christian religion. This was no easy task, as we shall see. The consolidation of the variations of gospels was difficult.

Gospels under consideration:

- Canonical Gospels of Matthew, Mark, Luke, John
- Gnostic Gospels of Thomas, Of Truth, Gospel of the Lord, Of the Egyptians, Nicodemus and Barnabas
- Partially preserved Gospels - Judas, Peter, Mary, Philip
- Fragmentary preserved Gospels - Dialogue of the Saviour, Papyrus Egerton 2, Gospel of Eve, Fayyum Fragment, Gospel of Mani, Oxyrhynchus Gospels, Gospel of the Saviour,

Gospel of the Twelve

- Gospels mentioned by early Christians, but not found - Bartholomew, the Seventy, the Four Heavenly Realms, of Perfection, Marcion, Basilides, Andrew, Apelles, Cerinthus, Bardesanes, of the Encratites, the Gnostics, Hesychius, Lucius, Longinus, Manes, Merinthus, Scythianus, Simonides, Tatian, Valentinus, Clementine
- And so on......

"Remember that what you are told is really three-fold; shaped by the teller; reshaped by the listener, concealed by both from the dead man of the tale."

- Vladimir Nabokov – The real life of Sebastian Knight

The outcome of the Council of Nicaea

- The New Testament was to include the Gospels of Mark, Matthew, Luke and John.
- Decrees issued by Bishops before Nicaea were collected into a Canon Law.
- The first version of the Nicene Creed was formulated.

Christology - The nature of Jesus

This was the most controversial issue. The debate was essentially reduced to two basic positions; both supported by scripture and therefore could not be reconciled:

- **Arian: Arius considered that Jesus was a finite being, and was under God the Father**. Quoting from Scripture, such as John 14:28: "*You heard me say, 'I am going away and I am coming back to you.' If you loved me, you would be glad that I am going to the Father, for the Father is greater than I*", and also Colossians 1:15: "*The Son is the image of the invisible God, the firstborn over all creation.*"
- **Alexander of Constantinople taught that the Son and the Father are equal.** Referring to scripture, such as John 10:30 "*I and the Father are one*" and John 17:21 "*That all of them may be one, Father, just as you are in me and I am in you. May they also be in us so that the world may believe that you have sent me*".

This disagreement demonstrates how difficult it is to resolve issues from inconsistent scriptures. Without concrete, independently verifiable facts, truth is hard to pin down.

There was no way to resolve the difference. To unify Christianity, Constantine saw little choice but to enforce one or other side of the argument.

Constantine favoured the Alexandrian version. Those who decided to vote against Alexander's version were threatened with banishment and excommunication. Not surprisingly, the final vote went overwhelmingly in favour of Alexander of Constantinople. Those who voted against the motion, including Arius, were excommunicated. Thus, Constantine enforced a unified Christianity and simultaneously created Heretics.

Emperor Constantine appointed himself as "Pontifex Maximus" which, in Roman law, was the chief priest of all religions. He established Christian orthodoxy by a council of bishops and enforced it by Imperial authority.

Constantine remained a polytheist, never converting to Christianity. Constantine's ongoing victorious battles were symbolized on structures, like bridges, with depictions of pagan gods such as Mithra, Apollo, Diana or Hercules, often omitting Christian references. When he dedicated the new capital of Constantinople to become the seat of Byzantine Christianity, he was wearing the Apollonian Diadem, a pagan symbol.

Constantine was no stranger to the exercise of terror either. For conspiring against him, he had his son Crispus killed by poisoning and his wife Fausta left to an agonising death in an overheated bath.[20],[21]

[20] Translation of the Zosimus - *Historia Nova* 1814
[21] Edward Gibbon, *The Decline and Fall of the Roman Empire*

Craving for Power

After the Council of Nicaea, Christianity enjoyed the recognition of Europe's most powerful emperor, who protected it against persecution and gave Christianity status from which to exercise influence and power. However, the Christian institution was far from united. It was organised according to the administrative structure of the Roman territories. This meant that the Church was thus divided into five Sees within the Empire and presided over by five Popes (also referred to as Patriarchs or Bishops). These Sees were Rome, Constantinople, Alexandria, Antioch, and Jerusalem.

The Emperors paid close attention to the appointment of Popes, often resulting in intense competition. Heresy was the weapon of choice in this battle for power. Ammunition was aplenty from Biblical passages that were used as gun fodder. The following passages, among others, can be used to question the nature of Jesus.

> John 14:28 - "You heard me say, 'I am going away and I am coming back to you.' If you loved me, you would be glad that I am going to the Father, for the Father is greater than I."
>
> **Matthew 27:46** - And about the ninth hour Jesus cried with a loud voice, saying, "Eli, Eli, lama sabachthani?", that is, "My God, my God, why hast thou forsaken me?"

Despite Constantine's efforts at unification, many sects of Christianity still existed such as:

Arianism. Arians believed that the Son of God was a Creature, made from nothing; and that he was God's First Production, before all ages. Arius (250–336 AD) argued that everything else was created through the Son.

Apollinarism, as per Apollinaris (before 390 AD), believed that Jesus could not have had a human mind but had a human body and soul but a divine mind.

Adoptionists believed that Jesus was adopted as God's son at his baptism.

Nestorians believed that Jesus had two natures, the Divine and the Human. Nestorius taught that the Son of God was altogether incapable of suffering, even within his union with the flesh, and that the Virgin Mary should be known as "Bringer forth of Christ" instead of "Bringer forth of God".

Novationists were Christians who followed the teachings of Pope Novatian. They believed that Christians who had not maintained their faith during persecution, should not be readmitted into communion with the Church.

Origenism, initially started by Origen Adamantius (184 – 253AD), taught that all human souls pre-existed and that souls which had been alienated from God because of sin, would by divine love and mercy, be ultimately reconciled with God. Origen is today regarded as one of the Church Fathers.

The Clash of Christian Patriarchs

Theophilus, Patriarch of Alexandria (Patriarch 385 – 412 AD)

The Alexandrian patriarchy had enjoyed high status, second only to the Roman patriarchy, but in 381 AD the Council of Constantinople declared the patriarchy of Rome and Constantinople equal, thus demoting the Alexandrian patriarchy from its former status to being under Constantinople. Patriarchs now had to compete for promotion to the status of the Patriarchy of Constantinople. The following events are a reflection of the aggressive clamouring for power and control.

Insecure of his status, the Alexandrian patriarch, Theophilus, persecuted the monks who had come under the influence of the Four Tall Brethren whom he accused of being heretic Origenists. With armed soldiers and servants, he attacked the defenceless monks, burned their dwellings, and "mis-treated" those he captured. Eastern Orthodox Christians honour a commemoration annually on July 10th for the 10,000 monks slain.

As a result, Theophilus was summoned by the Emperor to Constantinople in 402 AD to appear personally and apologize before a synod. The Patriarch of Constantinople, Chrysostom, was to preside over the charges brought against Theophilus by the Egyptian monks.

However, Theophilus appeared at Constantinople only a year later, accompanied by his nephew Cyril (who succeeded him ten years later) and twenty-eight loyal bishops and with large quantities of money and gifts. He took up residence in one of the palaces, and held conferences with all the adversaries of Chrysostom. Then he conferred with his own bishops and seven other bishops to concoct a long list of unfounded accusations against Chrysostom.

Chrysostom now found himself in the accuser's chair, eventually lost the case, and despite his support outside the synod, resigned to prevent bloodshed. Theophilus was never brought to justice and lived out his life in "ecclesiastic splendour" as Patriarch of Alexandria. Theophilus is now regarded as a saint by the Coptic Orthodox Church.

> "Theophilus...the perpetual enemy of peace and virtue, a bold, bad man, whose hands were alternately polluted with gold and with blood."

Edward Gibbon - The Decline and Fall of the Roman Empire

Cyril of Alexandria (Patriarch 412 – 444 AD)

Cyril was appointed Patriarch of Alexandria on 18 October 412 AD, succeeding his uncle Theophilus in the post despite riots between his supporters and those of his rival Timotheus. Cyril had established close ties with the Nitrian monks, having spent five years in ascetic training with them.

On his appointment, he immediately began to persecute Jews and plundered churches of Novatian Christians, whom he accused of being heretics. This brought him into direct confrontation with Orestes, the Roman Prefect of Alexandria and a Christian. The confrontation came to a head when Nitrian monks came out of the desert, instigated a riot and assaulted Orestes, accusing him of paganism. A stone, thrown by a member of the rioting crowd, hit Orestes on the head, resulting in severe bleeding. Orestes escaped further injury when the people of Alexandria rescued him. They caught the stone-thrower and chased the monks out of town. Subsequently, the stone-thrower was publicly tortured and killed. The aggravated confrontation between Orestes and Cyril reached a stalemate. Bishop Cyril sought a scapegoat.

Hypatia of Alexandria (370 – 415 AD)

Hypatia of Alexandria was an easy target. She headed the Platonist school at Alexandria and taught mathematics, philosophy and astronomy to various students, including pagans, Christians, and foreigners. A dignified and intelligent woman, Hypatia was frequently asked to give counsel on matters of state in a capacity usually reserved for men.

A contemporary church historian, Socrates Scholasticus, described her murder as follows:

> "Slanderous rumours circulated the Christian population that Hypatia stood in the way of a reconciliation between Orestes and the Bishop. Nitrian monks waylaid her on her way home, pulled her from her carriage and took her to the Caesareum church, stripped her, and dismembered her with broken tiles and oyster shells. When they had torn her body to pieces, they took her mangled limbs to Cinaron where they burned them. This awful behavior of Cyril reflected poorly on the whole Alexandrian church. Nothing can be farther from the spirit of Christianity than to allow behaviour such as massacres and fights. This incident happened in the fourth year after Cyril's appointment."
>
> - Socrates Scholasticus, Ecclesiastical History - Book VII Chapter XV.[22]

Orestes subsequently disappeared.

> "The mystical experience, the illumination, the great awakening, along with the charismatic seer who started the whole thing, are forgotten, lost, or transformed into their opposites. Organized Religion, the churches, finally may become the major enemies of the religious experience and the religious experiencer."
>
> - Abraham Maslow – Religion, Values and Peak Experiences

Further conflicts with Bishop Cyril and the Church

In 428 AD Nestorius, from Antioch, was appointed Archbishop of Constantinople which was senior over Alexandria, Bishop Cyril's domain. For Bishop Cyril this was disastrous, as he had persecuted Nestorians in Egypt ten years before. Cyril wrote a letter to the Egyptian monks accusing Nestorius of heresy. A copy of this letter reached Nestorius, who subsequently condemned it in his preaching. The interchange of letters between Cyril and Nestorius gradually escalated the hatred until Emperor Theodosius II called a council in Ephesus to resolve the dispute. Cyril began proceedings of the council in early 431AD before Nestorius' supporters from Antioch and

---

[22] Socrates Scholasticus, Ecclesiastical History - Book VII Chapter XV. - Translation is anonymous

Syria had arrived. Nestorius was therefore unable to defend himself. The council consequently ordered the deposition and exile of Nestorius for heresy.

However, when John, Patriarch of Antioch, and the other bishops finally reached Ephesus, they assembled their own council, condemned Cyril for heresy and deposed him from his see, labelling him as a *"monster, born and educated for the destruction of the church"*. The Emperor Theodosius II condemned Cyril for behaving like a "*proud pharaoh*" and reversed the verdict of the Council and arrested Cyril. However, he later escaped.

Cyril of Alexandria, was posthumously declared a Doctor of the Church in 1882 by Pope Leo XIII, a title reserved for certain Saints, known for the depth of understanding and orthodoxy of their theological teachings. His feast day is June 27th.

The Origin of Islam

Neo-Platonism and Christianity strongly influenced Islamic theology. There are many references to the Old Testament in the Quran and Islamic law (Sharia) is a variation of early Christian morality.

The Arabian Peninsula in the sixth century consisted, in the main, of a number of nomadic tribes. Although ignored by the conquests of the Vandals, Greeks, Romans and Mesopotamians, they were vulnerable to the organised militia of Europe. Uniting the Arabian Peninsula required a strong cultural and military identity.

Muhammad

Muhammad was born in 570 AD in the Arabian city of Mecca (Makka). Muslims teach that he restored the original monotheistic faith of Adam, Noah, Abraham and Moses.

Muhammad was orphaned at a young age and brought up by his uncle Abu Talib. While still in his teens, Muhammad accompanied his uncle on trading journeys to Syria where he became experienced in commercial trade, the only career open to Muhammad as an orphan. It is said that in his early teens, while accompanying a Meccan caravan to Syria, Muhammad met a Christian monk, Bahira who had a huge influence on the boy, predicting Muhammad's career as a prophet of God.

Muhammad became a merchant and transacted trade between the Indian Ocean and the Mediterranean Sea. At the age of 25, he married Khadijah, a forty-year-old widow.

Origins of the Quran

Early in his life Muhammad began a practice of meditating alone for several weeks every year in a cave on Mount Hira near Mecca. According to Islamic tradition, during one of his visits to Mount Hira in 610 AD, the angel Gabriel (Jibril) appeared to him and commanded Muhammad to recite the verses that were eventually to become the Qur'an. Until Muhammad's death, over a period of approximately 23 years, these revelations were memorized, recited and written down by Muhammad's companions. After Muhammad's death, the first Caliph Abu Bakr and other successors compiled the texts into a single book which became the basis of the Qur'an.

Uthman ibn Affan (653-656 AD) canonized his version of the Qur'an, and had other versions burnt. However, variations of the Qur'an still remained, such as the early manuscripts of the Umayyad and Abbasid Dynasties. The text of the Quran used today is taken from seven variant readings, out of fourteen, chosen by Ibn Mujahid and published as the Royal Cairo edition by King Fuad of Egypt.

"The Five Pillars of Islam" are the basic obligatory acts of faith in Islam. Summarized in the Hadith of Gabriel (Jibril) they are:

1. Shahada (to know and believe without suspicion, as if witnessed)
2. Salat (five daily prayers)
3. Zakāt (almsgiving)
4. Sawm (fasting during Ramadan)

5.   Hajj (pilgrimage to Mecca at least once in a lifetime)

The spread of Islam

Around 613 AD, Muhammad began preaching in public in Mecca, but was mostly ignored, mocked and eventually persecuted. In 615 AD he and his followers (about 40) were forced to flee Mecca. They escaped to the city of Yathrib, later renamed to "Medinat al-Nabi", (the City of the Prophet) or simply Medina. In 624, the Muslims, returning with a much larger army, won their first battle against the Meccans. This victory was seen as a sign that God (Allah) was on their side. However, the second battle was lost, Muhammad being wounded. In 630AD, Muhammad and his forces again marched to Mecca and this time they were victorious. The Ka'ba (Kaaba) temple was rededicated to Allah. By the time Muhammad died in 632AD, the entire Arabian Peninsula was under Muslim rule.

Caliphates

Muhammad had married several younger women since Khadijah's death; however, his only children were the daughters by Khadijah.

On his death, disagreement over the leadership of the Muslim community led to a number of civil wars.

Some followers, now called **Sunni Muslims**, maintained that the new leader should be elected from among those most capable. And so Prophet Muhammad's close friend and advisor, Abu Bakr was chosen.

Other followers, now called **Shia Muslims**, maintained that the leadership should stay within the close family and so their leadership passed directly to his cousin and son-in-law, Ali bin Abu Talib.

The resulting civil wars established a number of Caliphates. "Caliph" refers to a successor of the Muslim empires and is intended to be political and spiritual entities of the community of Muslim faithful, ruled by a Caliph. The Caliph is elected by officials who represent leaders of Islam and governed according to constitutional and religious law (Sharia). It was not unusual for a Caliph, who held the necessary military power, to be effectively self-appointed.

Expansion of Islam through the Caliphates

1st Caliph: (632 – 634) Abu Bakr quelled the rebellion and united Arabia. On his deathbed he appointed Umar ibn al-Khattab as his successor.

2nd Caliph: (634 – 644) Umar ibn al-Khattab expanded the Muslim empire into the greater Middle East. He was assassinated by a Persian in response to the Muslim conquest of Persia.

3rd Caliph: (644 – 656) Uthman ibn Affan was elected by a committee of six people and expanded the empire to North Africa and Central Asia but with much political cost. He also created a standardized version of the Qur'an. He was assassinated by the elite of Medina as a result of the rise of status and power of his clan.

4th Caliph: (656 – 661) the first Imam (religious leader), Ali ibn Abu Talib was elected after much persuasion. The A'isha, Talhah, Al-Zubayr and Umayyad tribes, especially Muawiyah I followers, wanted to take revenge for Uthman's death and punish the rioters who had killed him. They blamed Ali for not punishing the rebels and murderers of Uthman, the 3rd Caliph. A civil war ensued. The war ended indecisively. On Ali's assassination by Kharajiites (radical Muslims) the split between Shiite and Sunni factions became entrenched.

As the remnants of the Roman Empire remained divided, Caliphates grew stronger, invading the areas shown on the map.

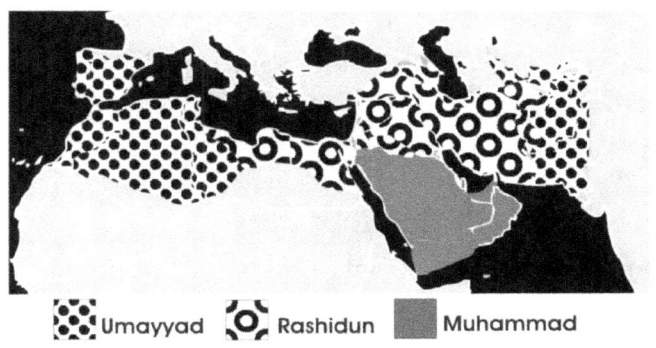

Umayyad **Rashidun** **Muhammad**

Caliphates actively promoted Islam in the process of expansion. Some Caliphates grew quickly, eventually invading the Iberian Peninsula up to the French town of Tours.

The Spread of Christianity

Charles Martel

(Charles the Hammer) (686 –741 AD). The Umayyad Caliphate had reached Tours in France via the Iberian Peninsula by 732, about 300 km from Paris. Charles Martel, the Frankish military and political leader of the region, drove back the Muslim invasion and won the Battle of Tours in 732, defeating the Caliphate army. This victory finally turned back the advance of Islam in the West. Charles Martel was the first to develop a system of feudalism and knighthood, which laid the foundation of a system of governance in the Carolingian Empire and eventually, most of the European continent. Charles Martel's son, Pepin the Short, finally reclaimed Southern France in 759.

Charlemagne (742 – 814 AD)

Charlemagne, grandson of Charles Martel, in 772 launched a 30-year military campaign to finalise the unification in Europe and succeeded in consolidating the regions, which are now France, Northern Italy and Germany. In response to the lingering influence of Islam, Charlemagne propagated Christianity in Europe by establishing monasteries throughout the empire. In 787, educational centres were added to all monasteries. The high calibre of the schools attracted scholars throughout Europe, England and Ireland.

Charlemagne condemned superstition and criticised clerics for "uncouth and unlettered tongues," and issued a directive to all the bishops and abbots to study. In the earliest known example of free education, he ordered every cathedral and monastery to allow both clergy and lay people access to learn, read and write without regard to their status. He ordered all to be treated equally to study grammar, music, arithmetic and medical knowledge.

This directive by Charlemagne propagated Christianity throughout Europe.

Holy Roman Empire

> "This agglomeration which was called and which still calls itself the Holy Roman Empire was neither Holy, nor Roman, nor an Empire."
> - Voltaire

The establishment of the Holy Roman Empire was a gradual process as German royalty succeeded emperors of Frankish origin. In 962 Otto I, a German, was crowned Emperor of the "Roman Empire", the first emperor of this domain who was not a member of the Carolingian dynasty.

The Emperors' Diminishing Divinity

Just as Constantine had placed himself at the head of the Church at Nicaea, emperors played a key role in the appointment of senior clerics. A close relationship between the Pope and the Emperor developed. The Pope would crown the Emperor and the Emperor would appoint the Pope, each validating the other. For the ordinary citizen it meant that both had apparent divine authority.

Change in perceptions occurred as the system of Fiefdoms, established by Charles Martel, proved to be a successful system of governance. Fiefdoms resolved issues of administration by delegating greater authority to the Barons, who kept land for the Emperor in return for a seat on the grand council by feudal tenure.

The feudal system consisted of property rights granted by an overlord (Baron) to a vassal, who held it in "fealty" in return for allegiance and service. These "fiefs" were often revenue-producing lands.

Fiefdoms were much smaller than the Roman provinces, thus lords of the fiefs enjoyed closer contact with the people of their domains, encouraging better oversight and control. Loyalty and bravery were rewarded with upward mobility and so it was possible for a peasant to become a knight.

Individuals of the fiefs, even slaves, could improve their status by developing their skills and knowledge. Cooking, entertainment, tailoring, shoe-making and military skills were always in demand and so people no longer felt trapped by their circumstances. Those who took ownership of their destiny honed their talents and skills to find paths of upward migration. This centered loyalties onto the lords of the fiefs.

Depending on the rank and tenure of the vassals, they could be called upon to advise Barons on matters of governance. A close working relationship between those working the fiefs and the Barons maintained the success of the system.

The Empire eventually resembled a federation of fiefdoms. The Barons of the fiefs were responsible for the production of food and utilities, collected taxes within their region and forwarded a portion of tax to the Emperor. The Emperors became increasingly dependent on the Barons.

The diminished authority of Emperors and Kings was demonstrated in 1100 when the feudal lords forced King Henry I of England to sign the Charter of Liberties binding the King to certain limitations in the treatment of church officials and nobles. This was followed by the signing of the Magna Carta of 1215, in which the King was forced to accept that he could no longer act arbitrarily. In 1338 the German princes proclaimed their right to choose the Emperor without papal intervention at the Diets of Rhense and Frankfurt.

As the power of the Barons of the fiefs increased, the validation of the Emperors' authority was no longer dependant on the Pope but gradually shifted to confirmation from the Barons. Consequently, the appointment of Popes by Emperors occupied a lower priority, often leaving rich and powerful families to influence the appointment of Popes.

A Troubled Papacy

Without the tight imperial control over the papacy, a number of bad popes made their appearance.[23] This raises questions of God's influence and interest in maintaining the integrity of the Church.

> **Pope Stephen VI** (896-897), was sponsored by the powerful Roman family, the house of Spoleto. He ordered his predecessor, Pope Formosus, to be exhumed, tried, de-fingered, briefly reburied, and then his corpse to be thrown into the Tiber River.

> **Sergius III** (904-11), Sergius III was lifted into power by the military commander Theophylact, Count of Tusculum. Sergius III murdered his predecessor. His cardinals called him "the slave of every vice". His teenage mistress Marozia, 30 years his junior, had an illegitimate son who grew up to become Pope John XI. Sergius III auctioned off top Vatican posts like trinkets.

> **Pope John XII** (937-964). Alberic II persuaded the Roman nobles in St. Peter's to promise, under an oath, that they would elect his son, Octavius, to the next vacant papal seat. Thus his son, Octavius, became Pope

---

[23] Russel Chamberlin – "Bad Popes"

John XII in 954 at the age of seventeen. As Pope he, together with his stepsister, Alda of Vienne, murdered people, blinded his confessor, gave land to a mistress, castrated and murdered one of his cardinals and turned the St. John Lateran palace into a brothel. A rampant paedophile, he performed regular sodomy with children, especially young boys, and claimed these acts to be an ancient Greek tradition. According to some sources, these acts were performed in major churches and often resulted in ritualised murder of his child victims. He was finally killed by a man who caught him in bed with his wife.

Benedict IX was in and out of office a number of times: Nephew of two preceding pontiffs, Pope Benedict VIII and Pope John XIX, he became Pope at a young age (18 or 20). Briefly forced out of Rome in 1036, he returned with the help of Emperor Conrad II.

In September 1044 he was forced out of the city again and John, Bishop of Sabina, was elected as Pope Sylvester III.

Benedict IX returned in April 1045 and expelled his rival, who however kept his claim to the papacy.

May 1045, Benedict IX resigned to get married. He sold his office to his godfather, John Gratian, who called himself Gregory VI.

Regretting his resignation, Benedict IX returned to Rome, taking the city and remained on the See until July

1046.

This time the German King Henry III intervened. At the Council of Sutri, December 1046, both Benedict IX and Sylvester III were deposed and Gregory VI (Benedict IX) resigned under pressure. The German Bishop Suidger was crowned Pope Clement II.

Benedict IX did not accept his enforced resignation and when Clement II died in October 1047, Benedict seized the Lateran Palace. However, he was forced out by German troops in July 1048 and Bishop Poppo of Brixen was elected as Pope Damasus II.

Benedict IX, (1032-48) also a paedophile, continually shocked his cardinals with his sexual acts involving young boys in St Lateran Palace (The Popes' Residence). According to Saint Peter Damian "He was a wretch who feasted on immorality."

Pope Victor III, referred to "his rapes, murders and other unspeakable acts. His life as a pope was so vile, so foul, so execrable, that I shudder to think of it."

Benedict IX was the first pope said to be homosexual and held orgies in the Lateran Palace.

Investiture Controversy: 1075

Churches and monastery buildings were considered the property of the fiefdoms. Barons applied principles of fiefs to church property and sold senior ecclesiastic posts in return for money and loyalty (Simony). These positions were sought after because of their high status, honour and influence. Many people within the church objected to this practice and an opportunity to oppose this custom arose when King Henry was appointed King at the age of six.

Pope Gregory VII in 1075 formally asserted in a collection of canons the "Dictatus Papae", that:

- The Roman church was founded by God alone.
- The papal power was the sole universal power.
- The deposal of an Emperor was under the sole power of the Pope.
- The Pope had the exclusive right to invest high clerics with insignia of office.

However, the implementation of these canons depended on certain Barons joining the fray against papal enemies. This led to a 50-year war, which ended with the Concordat of Worms in 1122. This agreement maintained the right of nobility to appoint church officials and the Pope to ratify these appointments. The Emperor was to be elected by the nobility and the Pope was to be elected by his cardinals. This agreement was a forerunner of the separation of Church and State and affirmed the freedom of the Church to act according to its own convictions.

A similar agreement was signed in England at the Concordat of London in 1107. However, corruption, misguided judgement and depravity persisted.

Pope Urban VI (1378-1389) complained that he did not hear enough screaming when cardinals who had conspired against him were tortured.

Pope Paul II (1464–1471) was alleged to have died of a heart attack while in a sexual act with a page.

Pope Alexander VI (1492-1503) had four children by his mistress (Vannozza dei Cattanei). His son Cesare, while only seventeen and a student, was made Archbishop of Valencia. Another son, Giovanni, received the dukedom of Gandia in Spain.

Pope Leo X (1513-1521), a spendthrift member of the Medici family, spent 14% of his predecessors' reserves on a single ceremony.

Pope Clement VII (1523-1534), a Medici, his inept power politicking with France, Spain, and Germany got Rome sacked, followed by many incidents of murder, rape and vandalism. Under his watch the Church of England was established when Henry VIII divorced Catherine of Aragon to marry Anne Boleyn.

Horror in the Dark Ages

"We must first confront our historical psychological actuality. And we must look into the abyss to be able to see beyond it."

~ Robert Jay Lifton -Theory of Thought Reform using Psychohistory.

Although much has been written about the Dark Ages, there is little analysis of the underlying elements leading to the atrocities of that period. This has restricted the ability to identify early warning signs, pointing to such tragedies.

Analysis reveals that certain actions of the Church in the Dark Ages are typical of any organisation vying for absolute power and dominance. Authoritarian institutions copy the mindset and belief systems that were rampant in the Dark Ages. Recent examples are Nazi Germany, Stalin's Russia, Pol Pot's Cambodia and a number of cults, such as Charles Manson (Helter Skelter)[24] and Jim Jones' People's Temple. Currently, Islamic extremism displays early warning signs, reminiscent of the Dark Ages.

---

[24] Bugliosi, Vincent with Gentry, Curt. *Helter Skelter — The True Story of the Manson Murders 25th Anniversary Edition*, W.W. Norton & Company, 1994. ISBN 0-393-08700-X.

The Catholic Church abolished inquisitional torture only in 1816. However many religious institutions today, still parade their autocratic posture.

The following events, as recorded by historians, are disturbing and may affect sensitive readers. We had debated the inclusion of this material for many months but finally decided for inclusion. No matter how upsetting the events are for us now, people who had suffered at the hands of such brutality, would very likely, want us to tell their stories, hoping that such attrocities should never occur again.

Sadly, because these events have not been sufficiently examined, many millions more people have suffered at the hands of extremism.

> "Facts do not cease to exist because they are ignored."
> ~Aldous Huxley

There is, in our culture, a notion to dismiss gross behaviour by way of semantic labels such as sociopathy, psychopathy, insanity or evil. In so doing, we avoid proper analysis and deprive ourselves of a deeper understanding of problem behaviour.

The following data will help us determine if there is an innate capacity in each person to breach the boundaries of a healthy personal ecology or, alternatively, if there are inherent elements in religion and autocratic regimes which lead to extremism.

> "I looked, and looked, and this I came to see:
> That what I thought was you and you,
> Was really me and me."
> ~ Ken Wilber, No Boundary: Eastern and Western Approaches to Personal Growth

The Crusades

Background

The Crusades are often romanticised as heroic quests to regain the Holy Land from the infidels (Muslims). History paints a different landscape. Not only were some of the Crusades absolute disasters, but they were often an indulgence in cruelty, greed and tyranny.

The history of the Crusades fills encyclopaedic volumes. Here we only examine events significant to our analysis with the aim of developing insight into the milieu affecting the Dark Ages.

After Muhammad's death, Islamic Caliphates had overrun the Iberian Peninsula. In 732 Charles Martel reversed the invasion. Charlemagne, his grandson, had consolidated the reversal of Muslim incursion by the time he was crowned "Emperor" by Pope Leo III on Christmas Day 800 AD.

However, Islamic Caliphates still threatened the eastern European front. The centre of the eastern Christian church, Byzantium (now Istanbul), fell in 1071 to the Seljuk Turks, cutting off the Christian route of pilgrimage to Jerusalem. Christian holy sites were desecrated and hermits persecuted.

The First Crusade (1096–1099)

The first Crusades was motivated in response to the Muslim advances on the eastern front, but quickly broadened out to include persecution of Jews, Mongols, other Christians such as Cathars, Hussites, Waldensians, Old Prussians, Pagans and political enemies of the Pope. To motivate aspirant crusaders, promises of absolution of their sins were made, by the Pope.

The trigger of this Crusade came from the Byzantine Emperor Alexios I, who found himself under pressure from invading Seljuk Turks. Alexios I appealed to Pope Urban II for assistance to stem the Turkish advance. Pope Urban II responded in 1096 with the primary goal of assisting Alexios, and re-conquering Jerusalem from Muslim rule soon became an additional goal.

The first target was Nicaea, which was successfully liberated by the Crusaders and handed over to Alexios. After a lengthy struggle for Antioch, it too was taken by the Crusaders in June 1098, but not before the Crusaders had massacred virtually all inhabitants, including Christians who were mistaken for Muslims.

The Crusaders then continued toward Jerusalem via Ma'arra. After the siege of Ma'arra, the Muslims surrendered. Again, the Crusaders massacred all inhabitants, an estimated 20,000. By this time, the Crusaders were hungry and malnourished.

> "In Ma'arra our troops boiled pagan adults in cooking pots and impaled children on spits and devoured them grilled".
> ~Ralph of Caen - Chaplin to the First Crusade

Most non-military personnel had been killed or had deserted. The remaining Crusaders arrived in Jerusalem and once inside, mercilessly slaughtered all inhabitants. Muslims and Jews were indiscriminately killed.

The Fourth Crusade (1202–1204)

> "There was never a greater crime against humanity than the Fourth Crusade."
> ~Sir Steven Runciman - "A History of the Crusades"

Jerusalem once more fell under Muslim control, this time under the Ayyubid dynasty centred in Egypt. Pope Innocent III motivated a new crusade; however, monarchs ignored the call until dramatic sermons by the French priest Fulk of Neuilly-sur-Marne, which persuaded lords of the fiefdoms to take action. The crusade aimed to free Jerusalem via Egypt, but instead invaded the Christian city of Constantinople, capital of the Eastern Roman Empire (Byzantium).

The Roman Pope Innocent III, although wishing to assert his authority over Byzantium, forbade the Crusaders from committing any atrocities against Eastern Orthodox Christians. This message was withheld from the Crusaders by Cardinal Peter of Capua, the papal legate, who encouraged an attack on Zara, a Christian town.

In the meantime, Alexios Angelos, whose father had been deposed as Byzantine emperor by his uncle Isaac III, financially sponsored the Crusade to regain Byzantium from his uncle. Alexios claimed that "the Greeks were worse than the Jews" and invoked the authority of God and the Pope to motivate the troops; even though the Pope had already demanded the end of the attack.

The Crusaders proceeded to sack Constantinople, capital of the Byzantine Empire and for three days, ruthlessly and systematically violated the city's churches and monasteries, destroying many ancient and medieval Roman and Greek works, including the Library of Constantinople, while stealing anything worthwhile.

Pope Innocent III angrily lamented:

> "How will the Greek Church ever return into an ecclesiastic union to a devotion for the Apostolic See when she has been so seriously persecuted by the Latins who acted with such dark perdition that now, with good

reason, they are more detested than dogs?

Those that were supposed to act in the name of Jesus Christ and not their own ends bloodied their swords with Christians instead of Pagans, not sparing religion, age or gender. They committed incest, adultery and fornication in the sight of men, exposed matrons and virgins, including those dedicated to God, to the sordid lusts of boys.

Not satisfied with theft of imperial treasure and those of nobility and lesser men, they also plundered the treasures of the church for their own gain, ripping silver plates from altars and hacking them into pieces to divide them among each other, violating holy places and stealing crosses and relics."

- Papal Letters, 126 (July 12, 1205) addressed to the papal legate, Cardinal Peter of Capua. [25]

Pope Innocent III excommunicated these Crusaders.

However, when the Crusaders took large amounts of money, priceless jewellery and valuables back to Rome, Pope Innocent III changed his mind and welcomed the stolen items, reversed their excommunication and recognised the installation of the Western prelates.

---

[25] Pope Innocent III, Ep 136, Patrologia Latina 215, 669-702, translation by James Brundage

"High ideals were besmirched by cruelty and greed ... the Holy War was nothing more than a long act of intolerance in the name of God".

~Sir Steven Runciman –"A History of the Crusades"

The Cathar (Albigensian) Crusade

Cathars had opposed the Catholic Church because of what they perceived to be moral, spiritual and political corruption. Catharism had spread across the Languedoc region, now south-west France. The Church's attempted peaceful conversion through debate, via the Dominicans, was unsuccessful. In 1208 the papal legate, Pierre de Castelnau, was murdered by a knight employed by Count Raymond of Toulouse. With an already tense situation, Pope Innocent III called for a crusade, declaring that all Albigenses "should be imprisoned and their property confiscated" and that the campaign "spared neither age nor sex".

Massacre of Beziers

The papal legate Abbot of Citeaux Arnaud Amalric was in command of the crusader army and besieged the town of Béziers on 22 July 1209. The Catholic inhabitants of the city were granted the freedom to leave unharmed, but many opted to stay and fight alongside the Cathars.

On 22 July 1209 the Cathars were overrun and the entire population of twenty thousand Cathars and Catholics were slaughtered. Thousands sought sanctuary in the Cathedral of St Nazaire which was subsequently burned down, resulting in the agonising death of all within. Others sought refuge in the Cathedral, the church of St Mary Magdalene and of St Jude. These and other churches were broken open, and all inside were slaughtered.

When the Crusaders asked how to distinguish Cathars from Catholics they were told by the Papal Legate Abbot of Citeaux Arnaud Amalric simply: *"Caedite eos! Novit enim Dominus qui sunt eius"* - **"Kill them all, God will recognize his Own"**. [26]

Arnaud Amalric subsequently wrote to Pope Innocent III, [27] "Today your Holiness, twenty thousand heretics were put to the sword, regardless of rank, age, or sex."

Atrocities following Beziers

Horror and terror spread throughout the Languedoc region. Many castles and towns offered little resistance. Carcassonne was attacked a month later and the citizens

---

[26] According to the Cistercian writer Caesar of Heisterbach
[27] the legate's own statement, in a letter to the Pope in August 1209

were forced, by Simon de Montfort, to leave the town naked.

Simon de Montfort was appointed leader of the crusading army and granted control of the area encompassing Carcassonne, Albi, and Béziers, making him the most important landowner of the region.

According to historians, Simon de Montfort was a man of extreme religious orthodoxy, notorious for his extreme cruelty, massacring whole towns. In Minerve he burned 140 Cathars who refused to give up their faith. He brought prisoners from the nearby village of Bram, had their eyes gouged out and their ears, noses and lips cut off. One prisoner, left with a single good eye, led the prisoners into the village as a warning.

Simon de Montfort had the full backing of the King of France, Philip Augustus. Although the King disapproved of the cruelty, he readily accepted the spoils.

Children's Crusade (1212-1213)

This was another tragically misguided event of the Crusades. In 1212, thousands of children between the ages of 10 to 18, mainly from Frankish and Germanic regions, set off to recapture Jerusalem. Some lower ranked nobles and clergy joined them. Many died crossing the Alps; others were captured and sold into slavery. Most of these children never reached Jerusalem.

"Oh my child where have you gone
We pray for you and wait
And wait we have too long
Oh God what have we done"

The Descent into Hell

"From the beginning men used God to justify the unjustifiable."

— Salman Rushdie, The Satanic Verses

The problem of Evil

Is God willing to prevent evil, but not able?	Then he is not omnipotent.
Is he able, but not willing?	Then he is malevolent
If he is both able and willing?	Then whence cometh evil?
If he is neither able nor willing?	Then why call him God?

- Epicurus [341-270 B.C.]

Islamist Extremism

The Dark Ages is about extremism in Christianity. By this stage Islam had been established for about 900 years. Pernicious Islamist terrorism against innocent people only occurs from the late 20th Century onward. The events of 9/11 are as fresh as yesterday and so are the Madrid train bombing 2004, Garage bomb in World Trade centre 1993, Suicide bombing in Bali October 2002, Bombing of

Synagogue Istanbul in 2003, Philippines bombings 2004, to name but a few.

There is a striking resemblance in the mindset and motivation of Islam and Christianity when we compare the Dark Ages with current Islamic extremism, pointing to common elements of extremism.

Christian Extremism

Since Nicaea, Popes, Bishops and Abbots enjoyed high profile and status including a lavish lifestyle equal to the nobility. Their wealth, power and influence often rivalled that of the nobility.

The increasing success of the feudal system meant that the papacy could no longer rely on the Emperor alone for support, but also needed the backing of the increasingly powerful feudal Barons. In a more complex political environment, new Christian sects emerged, supported by local barons. The loss of influence by the Roman Church, in these fiefdoms, threatened its dominance, status and ultimately its existence. In addition, there was a growing threat from the Islamic Caliphates on the Byzantine borders.

In its fight for survival, the papacy enrolled a number of Kings and Barons as legates[28] to represent it against the emerging sects considered heretic

For the Church to reach its political aim of restoring its supremacy, the Inquisitions were established. The methods used by the inquisitors often involved ingenious methods of torture to drive fear and trepidation into the hearts of the populace.

Popes were actively involved in promulgating the Inquisitions and Witch Hunts by creating the infrastructure and the moral framework.

> "Anyone who attempts to construe a personal view of God which conflicts with Church Dogma must be burned without Pity".
> - Pope Innocent III

Inquisition Popes

- **Innocent III** (1161-1198), a vigorous opponent of heresy, undertook many campaigns against it. Initially he focused on the Albigenses, also known as the Cathars. This led to the infamous massacre of Bezier and other atrocities.
- **Pope Gregory IX** (1227 to 1241) formalised the Inquisitions with a series of Papal Bulls. This system became known as the Papal Inquisition.

---

[28] A Legate is "An ordinary and permanent representative of the Pope, vested with both political and ecclesiastical powers, accredited to the court of a sovereign or assigned to a definite territory with the duty of safeguarding the interests of the Holy See."

- **Pope Innocent IV** (1243 to 1254) issued the Papal Bull "Ad extirpanda", which authorized the use of torture by the Inquisition for eliciting confessions from heretics. It states "heretics are murderers of souls as well as robbers of God's sacraments and of the Christian faith ...to be coerced—as are thieves and bandits—into confessing their errors and accusing others, although one must stop short of danger to life or limb".

- **Pope Paul III** (Pope from 1534 to 1549) established a system of tribunals, administered by the "Supreme Sacred Congregation of the Universal Inquisition", staffed by cardinals and other Church officials. This system became known as the Roman Inquisition.

Theology of Extremism

Two men were walking down a street in their neighbourhood when they noticed a building which had been repainted.

X: "Turquoise is not a nice colour for that building"
Y: "That's not Turquoise; it's Aquamarine and it's perfect"
X: "No, that's Turquoise"
Y: "No, that's Aquamarine"
X: Can you prove it?"
Y: Pulls out a gun and shoots X
X: Sinks to the ground, mortally wounded. "Why do you kill me?"
Y: "To prove that I am right"

This rather crass example illustrates the foolishness of efforts to suppress ideas. An idea that occurs in one mind can occur in many others. Eliminating the person does not eliminate the Idea.

"The suppression of uncomfortable ideas may be common in religion or in politics, but it is not the path to knowledge, and there's no place for it in the endeavor of science. We do not know beforehand where fundamental insights will arise about our mysterious and lovely solar system.
The history of our study of our solar system shows us clearly that accepted and conventional ideas are often

wrong, and that fundamental insights can arise from the most unexpected sources."

-- Carl Sagan, Cosmos television series

Heresy, Blasphemy, Apostasy and more

An idea, when debated, either becomes stronger and more robust *or* it expires. Debate strengthens aspects that have value and trims away aspects without substance. The result is an idea that adds to humanity's wellbeing. When an idea does not go through a process of criticism, it remains immature and vulnerable.

Heresy, Blasphemy, Apostasy and other attempts at limiting ideas, are self-defeating.

Heresy

Heresy in Christianity

Heresy: "an infidelity in men who, having professed the faith of Christ, corrupt its dogmas".

St. Thomas Aquinas (Summa II-II:11:1) 1225 –1274

The first known usage of the term "Heresy" in a legal context began after Nicaea, in 380 AD by the Edict of Thessalonica of Theodosius I, which made Christianity the State church of the Roman Empire. Prior to the Edict, the Church had no state-sponsored support for or legal mechanism to counter what it perceived as "heresy". By this edict the State's authority and that of the Church became merged. One of the outcomes of this merging was the sharing of State powers for legal enforcement with Church authorities. This reinforcement gave Church leaders the power to pronounce the death sentence for Heresy.

Heresy in Islam

Muslims referred to heretics and those who antagonized Islam as *zindiqs*, the charge being punishable by death.

One recent example is the fatwa issued by Iran, offering a reward for anyone who succeeded in assassinating the author Salmon Rushdie for his writings including the "Satanic Verses".

The two main streams of Islam, Sunnis and Shi'as, have regarded each other as heretics. Others see Ismailis, the Hurufiya, the Alawis, the Bektashi, the Salafi and the Sufis as heretics. Sufism is tolerated by some Shi'a and Sunnis, but the new movement of Wahhabism considers it heretical.

Blasphemy

Blasphemy is irreverence toward holy persons, artefacts, customs, and beliefs, irrespective of one's own beliefs of religion.

Blasphemy in Christianity

"Compare murder and blasphemy as objects of the two sins, it is clear that blasphemy, which is a sin committed directly against God, is more grave than murder, which is a sin against one's neighbour.

On the other hand, if we compare them in respect of the harm wrought by them, murder is the graver sin, for murder does more harm to one's neighbour, than blasphemy does to God."

- Thomas Aquinas' Summa Theologiae

Blasphemy in Islam

Quran Surat 5:33 "Those who wage war against Allah and His Messenger, and go about the earth spreading mischief - indeed their recompense is that they either be done to death, or be crucified, or have their hands and feet cut off from the opposite sides or be banished from the land. Such shall be their degradation in this world; and a mighty chastisement lies in store for them in the World to Come"

Kuwait's parliament, in May 2012, approved a law that calls for the death penalty for insulting Allah, the Prophet Muhammad, his wives and relatives, in a sign of the growing influence of Islamist extremism.

Apostasy

Apostasy is the disaffiliation, abandonment or renunciation of a religion. In Islam, it attracts the death penalty.

Apostasy in Christianity

King James Version, Deuteronomy 13

"6 If thy brother, the son of thy mother, or thy son, or thy daughter, or the wife of thy bosom, or thy friend, which is as thine own soul, entice thee secretly, saying, Let us go and serve other gods, which thou hast not known, thou, nor thy fathers;

7 Namely, of the gods of the people which are round about you, nigh unto thee, or far off from thee, from the one end of the earth even unto the other end of the earth;

8 Thou shalt not consent unto him, nor hearken unto him; neither shall thine eye pity him, neither shalt thou spare, neither shalt thou conceal him:

9 But thou shalt surely kill him; thine hand shall be first upon him to put him to death, and afterwards the hand of all the people.

10 And thou shalt stone him with stones, that he die; because he hath sought to thrust thee away from the LORD thy God, which brought thee out of the land of Egypt, from the house of bondage.

11 And all Israel shall hear, and fear, and shall do no more any such wickedness as this is among you.

12 If thou shalt hear say in one of thy cities, which the LORD thy God hath given thee to dwell there, saying,

13 Certain men, the children of Belial, are gone out from among you, and have withdrawn the inhabitants of their city, saying, Let us go and serve other gods, which ye have not known;

14 Then shalt thou inquire, and make search, and ask diligently; and, behold, if it be truth, and the thing certain, that such abomination is wrought among you;

15 Thou shalt surely smite the inhabitants of that city with the edge of the sword, destroying it utterly, and all that is therein, and the cattle thereof, with the edge of the sword.

16 And thou shalt gather all the spoil of it into the midst of the street thereof, and shalt burn with fire the city, and all the spoil thereof every whit, for the LORD thy God: and it shall be an heap for ever; it shall not be built again.

17 And there shall cleave nought of the cursed thing to thine hand: that the LORD may turn from the fierceness of his anger, and show thee mercy, and have compassion upon thee, and multiply thee, as he hath sworn unto thy fathers;

18 When thou shalt hearken to the voice of the LORD thy God, to keep all his commandments which I command thee this day, to do that which is right in the eyes of the LORD thy God."

127

Apostasy in Islam

The Quran

4:89 - "They but wish that ye should reject Faith, as they do, and thus be on the same footing (as they): But take not friends from their ranks until they flee in the way of Allah (From what is forbidden). But if they turn renegades, seize them and slay them wherever ye find them"

9:11-12 - "But if they repent and establish worship and pay the poor-due, then are they your brethren in religion. We detail our revelations for a people who have knowledge. And if they break their pledges after their treaty (hath been made with you) and assail your religion, then fight the heads of disbelief - Lo! they have no binding oaths - in order that they may desist."

4:80 - "Whoso obeyeth the Messenger obeyeth Allah."

The Hadith - regarded as a source of Islamic jurisprudence:

Bukhari (52:260) - "...The Prophet said, 'If somebody (a Muslim) discards his religion, kill him.'

Bukhari (84:57) - [In the words of] "Allah's Apostle, 'Whoever changed his Islamic religion, then kill him.'"

Bukhari (89:271) - A man who embraces Islam, then reverts to Judaism is to be killed according to "the verdict of Allah and his apostle."

Bukhari (84:64-65) - "Allah's Apostle: 'During the last

days there will appear some young foolish people who will say the best words but their faith will not go beyond their throats (i.e. they will have no faith) and will go out from (leave) their religion as an arrow goes out of the game. So, wherever you find them, kill them, for whoever kills them shall have reward on the Day of Resurrection.'"

Reliance of the Traveller (Islamic Law) o8.1 - "When a person who has reached puberty and is sane voluntarily apostasizes from Islam, he deserves to be killed."

Honour Killings

In modern history, honour killings occur mainly in Muslim countries such as Jordan, Syria, Saudi Arabia and Pakistan but also in India where there is a strong Islamic influence.

"Women in Pakistan live in fear. They face death by shooting, burning or killing with axes if they are deemed to have brought shame on the family. They are killed for supposed 'illicit' relationships, for marrying men of their choice, for divorcing abusive husbands. They are even murdered by their kin if they are raped as they are thereby deemed to have brought shame on their family. The truth of the suspicion does not matter -- merely the allegation is enough to bring dishonour on the family and therefore justifies the slaying."

"Amnesty International calls on the Government of Pakistan to take urgent measures in the following three areas in fulfillment of its obligation to provide effective protection to women against violence perpetrated in the name of honour and to end the impunity currently enjoyed by its perpetrators". [29]

Children of Muslim parents, who migrated to the Western world, spontaneously assimilate into the new Western culture. Some Muslim parents kill their child, especially girls who reject arranged marriages for romantic love. Known as 'Honour Killing', parents who feel 'disgraced' by their daughter's romantic choice of a husband, must kill their child, according to the dictates of their religion.[30]

---

[29] Honour killings of girls and women – Amnesty International 1999 – AI index ASA 33/18/99
[30] www.mindandreligion.com

The Inquisitions

"There has been no more organized effort by a religion to control people and contain their spirituality than the Christian Inquisition. Developed within the Church's own legal framework, the Inquisition attempted to terrify people into obedience."

- Helen Ellerbe -"The Dark Side of Christian History"

We focus on the early Church because there is abundant data. However, the systems of abuse are by no means limited there. We find such beliefs, dormant, in many Christian and Islamic sects, New Age Religions and authoritarian regimes such as Nazi Germany, Stalin's Soviet Union and Pol Pot's Cambodia.

In discussing the events of the Crusades, Inquisitions and Witch Hunts, we are identifying systemic elements that propagate destructive beliefs. The horrors of the Inquisitions and Witch Hunts were not the result of the actions of a few mentally ill individuals, but rather a system of socialised beliefs and motives.

Inquisitions and Witch Hunts were fear-driven purges against all who questioned the dogma of its religion. The ferocity of its methods reflects the intense existential anxiety often felt by religious leaders. The Dark Age was a war of ideas. Such a war cannot be won by murder or torture.

The Languedoc Inquisition

After the atrocities at Beziers, described earlier, the first Inquisition was temporarily established in 1184 in Languedoc (south-west of France) to remove the resilient threat of Cathars (Albigensians). It was permanently established in 1229 under the Dominicans in Rome and was later moved to Carcasonne.

Local authorities in Languedoc established a tribunal to prosecute heretics. After 1200AD, a Grand Inquisitor headed each Inquisition. These Inquisitions remained active into the 19th century.

A 1578 handbook for Inquisitors explained the purpose of inquisitorial penalties: "... for punishment does not take place primarily for the correction and good of the person punished, but for the public good so that others may become terrified and weaned away from the evils they would commit."

The Inquisition uprooted the remaining Cathars in the south at Toulouse, in the regions of Albi, Carcassonne.

Between May 1243 and March 1244, the Cathar fortress of Montségur was besieged by the troops of the

Archbishop of Narbonne in Carcassonne. On 16 March 1244 a symbolically important massacre took place, where over 200 Cathar monks were burnt in one enormous fire near the foot of the castle. The region was finally "cleansed" of Catharism, those who refused to recant were hanged, or burnt at the stake.

The Spanish Inquisition (1480 - 1834)

After the defeat of the last Muslim Caliphate in Granada in 1492, the entire Iberian Peninsula was brought back under Christian dominion. A tribunal had been established in 1480 by the Spanish Catholic Monarchs, Ferdinand II of Aragon and Isabella I of Castile, to "*cleanse religion*" in their kingdoms, and to take control of the Inquisitions which had been under papal control.

Torquemada, the confessor of Queen Isabella, was appointed the Grand Inquisitor of Spain from 1483. In the fifteen years under his direction, the Spanish Inquisition grew from one tribunal at Seville to a network of twenty-four 'Holy Offices'. The use of torture was intensified if the accused refused to confess. Torquemada showed no mercy to those who refused to repent. Many people were thrown into prison and remained there until they died. Many others were either publicly beheaded or burned at the stake. It is estimated that in the period until Torquemada's death some 2000 people were killed. Anyone who spoke against the Inquisition became a suspect and could face the same fate as the accused – as did Saint Teresa of Ávila and Saint John of the Cross.

Royal decrees issued in 1492 and 1501 ordered Jews and Muslims to convert or leave Spain. The Jewish plight was already dire as mobs attacked, killed and destroyed their property in the 1391 riots in Seville, Valladolid and Barcelona. These attacks were instigated by the hate sermons preached by various priests. Mass conversions of Jews and Muslims to Christianity followed. However, scepticism persisted concerning the authenticity of these conversions and "Conversios" continued to suffer discrimination, persecution and torture.

Auto-da-fé

These were public processions of the "guilty" and a reading-out of their sentences. It included a Catholic Mass and prayer. They took place in public esplanades lasting many hours, church and civil authorities attending. The first was held in Seville in 1481 where six people were burned alive. Rapid expansion of the tribunals followed in Castile. By 1492 they were established in Ávila, Córdoba, Jaén, Medina del Campo, Segovia, Sigüenza, Toledo, and Valladolid.

The Plight of the Waldensians

The founder Peter Waldo (1140 – 1218) strongly condemned papal excesses and Catholic dogmas, including purgatory and transubstantiation. (The miracle of the substance of the bread and the wine in the sacrament is changed into the substance of the Body and the Blood of Jesus.)

Waldensians (Waldenses or Vaudois): Although they considered themselves Christians, their interpretations of Christianity were forbidden by Pope Alexander III. They nevertheless continued to preach according to their own understanding of the scriptures.

In 1184 Pope Lucius III formally declared Waldensians as heretics and this was restated by Pope Innocent III in 1215.

A number of incidents followed:

- In 1212, 80 Waldensians were caught and burned in Strasbourg.
- In 1332, Inquisitors purged heretics from the valleys of Perosa (now Switzerland).
- In 1393, the Inquisitor Borelli burned more than 150 men, women, girls, and young children, in a single day in Dauphine.
- Christmas 1400, a general slaughter of the inhabitants of Pragelas was ordered. Many who fled, perished in the snow, dead children clasped in the frozen arms of their mothers.
- Pope Innocent VIII in 1487 recruited some 36,000 men to crush the Waldensians "like venomous snakes." 18,000 troops plus an equivalent number of criminals and desperados

assembled to slaughter the Waldensians in the Alps, one village after another.

- As a reward, these criminals and desperados were absolved from their sins and property stolen was legitimised if they killed a heretic. Pope Innocent VIII annulled all Waldensian contracts, and forbade anyone from giving them aid of any kind and gave everyone permission to take their property.

Massacre of Mérindol

Once again, this time in 1545, Francis I, King of France, ordered the purging of Waldensian heresy. Subsequently, Jean Maynier d'Oppède and Antoine Escalin des Aimars led an attack on the defenceless Waldensian farming community in the Piedmont valley, northern Italy today.

The soldiers attacked the village of Mérindol and devastated neighbouring Waldensian villages. Captured men were sent into forced labour on French galleys. About 25 villages were destroyed. Thousands of people were killed.

For these deeds, Pope Paul III rewarded Jean Maynier d'Oppède with imperial honours.

Massacre of La Torre (1655)

Fearful that these atrocities would be hard to believe, Pastor Leger set out to record these deeds for posterity, by providing a clear, irrefutable, and unquestionable proof of these awful crimes.[31] He travelled from one community to the other, immediately after the massacre, with notaries who took down the depositions and attestations of survivors and eye-witnesses. From the evidence, he compiled the book "Histoire Generale des EglisesEvangeliques des Vallees de Piemontou Vaudoises".

The accompanying images are from Sir Samuel Morland - "The history of the evangelical churches of the valleys of Piemont 1658".

> Jean Leger writes:-
>
> "At four o'clock on the morning of Saturday, the 24th of April, 1655, the signal was given from the castle-hill of La Torre. .... On the instant a thousand assassins began the work of death. Dismay, horror, agony, woe in a moment overspread the Valleys of Lucerna and Angrogna. "

---

[31] These accounts are related by Jean Leger, pastor and moderator of the Waldensian Church, 1669 in "Histoire Generale des Eglises Evangeliques des Vallees de Piemontou Vaudoises" and translated by the late Rev. W. S. Gilly, D.D., Canon of Durham and J. Aldensian Wylie (1808-1890)

".... a priest and monk accompanied each party of soldiers, to set fire to the houses as soon as the inmates had been dispatched. Alas! what sounds are those that repeatedly strike the ear? The cries and groans of the dying were echoed and re-echoed from the rocks around, and it seemed as if the mountains had taken up a wailing for the slaughter of their children.

"Our Valley of Lucerna," exclaims Leger, "which was like a Goshen, was now converted into a Mount Etna, darting forth cinders and fire and flames. The earth resembled a furnace, and the air was filled with a darkness like that of Egypt, which might be felt, from the smoke of towns, villages, temples, mansions, granges, and buildings, all burning in the flames of the Vatican" [Leger, part ii., p. 113].

Soldiers were not content with a quick kill; they invented new and gruesome methods of torture and death. It is difficult to write in plain words all the disgusting and horrible deeds of these men; their wickedness can never be all known, because it is too gruesome to be told.

From the awful narration of Leger, we select only a few instances; but even these few, however mildly stated, grow, without our intending it, into a group of horrors. Little children were torn from the arms of their mothers, clasped by their tiny feet, and their heads smashed against the rocks; or were held between two soldiers and their quivering limbs torn up by main force. Their mangled bodies were then thrown on the highways or fields, to be devoured by beasts. The sick and the aged were burned alive in their dwellings. Some had their hands and arms and legs lopped off, and fire applied to the severed parts to staunch the bleeding and

prolong their suffering. Some were flayed alive, some were roasted alive, some disemboweled; or tied to trees in their own orchards, and their hearts cut out. Some were horribly mutilated, and of others the brains were boiled and eaten by these cannibals. Some were fastened down into the furrows of their own fields, and

141

ploughed into the soil as men plough manure into it. Others were buried alive. Fathers were marched to death with the heads of their sons suspended round their necks. Parents were compelled to look on while their children were first outraged, then massacred, before being themselves permitted to die. But here we must stop.

Farther in Leger's narration continues, but we end it here. There come vile, abominable, and monstrous deeds, utterly and overwhelmingly disgusting, horrible and fiendish, which we dare not transcribe. The heart sickens, and the brain begins to swim. "My hand trembles," says Leger, "so that I scarce can hold the pen, and my tears mingle in torrents with my ink, while I write the deeds of these children of darkness—blacker even than the Prince of Darkness himself" [Leger, part ii., p. 111].

No general account, however awful, can convey so correct an idea of the horrors of this persecution as would the history of individual cases; but this we are precluded from giving. We could describe these cases, with hundreds of others equally horrible and appalling, our narrative would grow so harrowing that our readers, unable to proceed, would turn from the page. Literally did the Waldenses suffer all the things of which the apostle speaks, as endured by the martyrs of old, with other torments not then invented, or which the rage of even a Nero shrank from inflicting?

"These cruelties form a scene that is unparalleled and unique in the history of at least civilized countries. There have been tragedies in which more blood was spilt and more life sacrificed, but none in which the actors were so completely dehumanised, and the forms of suffering so monstrously disgusting, so unutterably cruel and revolting. The Piedmontese Massacres in this respect stand alone. They are more fiendish than all the atrocities and murders before or since, and Leger may still advance his challenge to "all travelers, and all who have studied the history of ancient and modern pagans, whether among the Chinese, Tartars and Turks, they ever witnessed or heard tell of such execrable perfidies and barbarities."

"Uncontrollable grief seized the hearts of the survivors at the sight of their brethren slain, their country devastated, and their Church overthrown. "Oh that my head were waters," exclaims Leger, "and mine eyes a fountain of tears, that I might weep day and night for the slain of the daughter of my people! Behold and see if there be any sorrow like unto my sorrow." "It was then," he adds, "that the fugitives, who had been snatched as brands from the burning, could address God in the words of the 79th Psalm, which literally as emphatically describes their condition:--"

"'O God, the heathen are come into thine inheritance,

Thy holy temple have they defiled;
They have laid Jerusalem on heaps.
The dead bodies of thy servants have they given
To be meat unto the fowls of heaven,
The flesh of thy saints unto the beasts of the earth,
Their blood have they shed like water;...
And there was none to bury them!'"
[Leger, part ii., p. 113].

I don't know if God exists, but it would be better for His reputation if He didn't.
Jules Renard - French author

St Bartholomew's Day Massacre

Catherine de' Medici, in 1560, became regent on behalf of her ten-year-old son King Charles IX and was granted sweeping powers as legate of the Pope, given both political and ecclesiastical powers with the duty of safeguarding the interests of the Holy See. An uneasy peace had existed between Catholics and Huguenots since the peace treaty of Saint-Germain-en-Laye in 1570 to end the third religious war. This tension reached breaking point after the attempted assassination of Admiral de Coligny on 22 August 1572.

Trusting the French monarchy, many French Huguenots had gathered in Paris for the wedding of Henry of Navarre and Catherine's daughter, Margaret of Valois. However, Catherine de Medici had conspired a general massacre of the Huguenot leaders. The gates of the city were locked, and then the soldiers attacked the, mainly unarmed, Huguenots. Coligny and all leaders were killed first. Thereafter, all Huguenots that the King's Swiss Guard and mob could find were massacred. In Paris the massacre lasted for three days and spread from there into other areas of France such as the provinces of Rouen, Lyons, Bourges, Orleans, and Bordeaux. An estimated 3,000 were killed in Paris and up to 70,000 in all of France.

The Pope and the King of Spain welcomed the news of these massacres. Protestants, however, were horrified, and the killings rekindled the hatred between Protestants and Catholics and resulted in the resumption of the war.

On hearing of the massacre, Pope Gregory XIII ordered a jubilee in celebration and recruited Vasari to include commemorative scenes of the victory of "the most Christian King" over the Huguenots, on one of the paintings in a Vatican apartment. He also had a medal struck representing an exterminating angel killing the Huguenots with his sword with the inscription: "*Ugono-torum strages*" (Huguenot mass slaughter). He sent a

Golden Rose to the King as a token of reverence and ordered a "Te Deum" to be sung as a special thanksgiving.

Witch Hunts

Consequences of Irrational Ideas

"Thou shalt not suffer a witch to live."
Exodus 22.18

Witch hunts cry out for proper analysis, understanding and reform. Persecutions, based on religious beliefs, are still practised to this day, in many parts of the world.

The following narrations emphasise the need for factual evidence. Religion is a perfect nest for superstitions; neither able, or willing to seek out independently verifiable facts to support their beliefs.

The Inquisitors possessed a need to inflict as much pain and suffering as possible on their fellow human beings. Which begs the question: "What is evil?"

Very often, the torture did not end with a confession. Those who confessed were burned alive or thrown into jail where they died of hunger and neglect. Survivors suffered permanent physical and mental trauma. It is painfully obvious that people (guilty or not) will confess to anything under the kind of torture described below.

The Inquisitions brought about irrational tyranny to every corner of Europe, triggering the fear of sorcery and witchcraft as it made its way into the darkened minds of people, especially the clergy. These fears resonate with religious tenets such as "Evil" and "Satan" and create moral panic. Phobias grew fastest among the clergy until in 1320 Pope John XXII authorized the Inquisitions to persecute witchcraft for "heresy".

Legality of Witch Hunts

The torture of witches grew after 1468 when Pope Paul II declared witchcraft to be "crimen exeptum", setting aside the legal limits (such as they were) on the application of torture when evidence was difficult to find.

In 1376 Nicholas Eymerich published the *"Directorium Inquisitorum"* a treatise on witchcraft, describing the means for discovering witches using confiscated magic texts from accused "sorcerers". This treatise was highly influential in determining the conduct during massacres in the Albigensian and subsequent crusades.

The newly invented Gutenberg printing press provided a German Catholic inquisitor, Heinrich Kramer, with an opportunity to spread witch-phobia with his 1486 treatise, "**Malleus Maleficarum**" (The Witch Hammer), which "proved" that witchcraft existed and instructed magistrates in procedures to find and convict witches.

"Proof" of Witchcraft included:

- Moles, birthmarks or "<u>invisible</u>" physical markings
- Unusual achievements were seen as evidence of a pact with the Devil in return for some worldly talent.
- Denouncement by another victim under torture
- Friendship with other witches
- Blasphemy
- Participation in a Coven (gatherings of witches)
- Casting of spells
- Possession of objects of witchcraft
- Witches in the family
- Showing fear during the interrogations
- Not crying during torture
- Sexual relationships with a demon

Torture became the modus operandi to 'extract confessions' and to force disclosure of names of 'collaborating witches'. It is very likely that, to escape further pain and degradation, victims would utter the names of anyone who came to mind. Innocent people (mostly women) were burned at the stake, drowned or hanged, many more were tortured.

Instruments of Torture

Under the eye of the all-seeing, all-powerful, compassionate God

"Men never do evil so completely and cheerfully as when they do it from religious conviction."
- Blaise Pascal (1623-1662)

Torture tools used are indicative of the depravity of the Inquisitions. A selection is on view at The Medieval Torture Museum, San Gimignano, Italy.

Head Crusher. With the head placed under the upper cap and the chin placed above the bottom bar, the top screw of the device was slowly turned, compressing the skull. First the teeth are destroyed, shattering and splintering into the jaw. Then the eyes are squeezed from the sockets – some versions had special receptacles to catch them. Lastly, the skull fractures and the brain is forced out. To prolong the torture, the torturer could keep the head firmly clamped and strike the metal skullcap periodically, each blow echoing pain throughout the victim's body.

The Cradle. The victim was hung with an iron belt

surrounding his upper waist, bound hand and foot; legs kept slightly open by a stick in such a way that he could only move them at the same time. He was hoisted over a pointed pyramid put on top of a rack. His legs were stretched out to the front and joined with a rope at his ankles. The victim was lowered onto a pyramid point that penetrated into the anus or vagina and was kept in this position until the victim confessed.

The Virgin of Nuremberg. A sarcophagus was fitted with spikes on the inside that pierced different parts of the body but never injured vital organs in order to keep the victim alive, hanging upright. The device would be opened both from the front and from the back without the victim being able to get out. The container was so thick that screaming could not be heard from the outside.

The Saw. The victims were hung upside down by their feet and then sawed in half from the crotch. The inverted position of the victim meant that blood flow to the head increased the duration of awareness of the increasing pain during this gruesome death.

Breast Ripper Used as a way to punish women, the breast

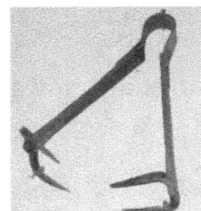 ripper was a painful and cruel way to mutilate a woman's breasts. This instrument was used on women accused of conducting a miscarriage or adultery.

The claws were used either hot or cold on the victim's exposed breasts. If the victim wasn't killed she would be scarred for life as her breasts were literally torn apart.

A frequent variation of the breast ripper is often referred to as "The Spider" which is a similar instrument attached to a wall. The victim's breasts were fixed to the claws and the woman was pulled by the torturer away from the wall; removing them.

The Pear, shaped like a pear, this instrument had a screw by which it could be expanded. It was forced into the mouth or rectum of male victims or into the vagina of female victims. The instrument was then expanded. The oral, rectal, or vaginal pear was used on people guilty of sodomy, on women guilty of adultery, people guilty of incest or sexual union with Satan, and it was also used on heretical preachers and "blasphemers".

The Inquisitional Chair was covered with spikes on the back, armrests, seat, leg-rests and footrests. The spikes were designed to pierce the victim's body. A screw bar would immobilize the victim and make the pins penetrate more deeply. The seat, made of iron, could be heated.

Cat's Paw. This instrument had very long and sharp claws. It was used to rip the victim's flesh to shreds. Muscles and bones were no obstacle.

The Mask. The victims were staked out to public ridicule and at the same time they were physically tortured. The masks sometimes had inner devices, such as a ball, which were forced into the victim's mouth, thus preventing screaming.

The Fork. This instrument was made of two little forks, one set against the other and of which the points rammed into the flesh under the chin and over the chest. A little collar supported the instrument to prevent any movement of the victim. The forks did not penetrate into vital points, prolonging suffering before death.

THE RACK.

The Rack consisted of a rectangular, usually wooden frame, slightly raised from the ground, with a roller at one, or both, ends. The victim's feet were attached to one roller, and the wrists to the other. The rollers could be rotated, thus straining the sufferer's joints until they were dislocated and finally ripped off.

Intestinal Crank. An incision was made in the abdominal area, cutting the upper intestine from the stomach and attaching it to a crank. The crank then would be rotated to extract the intestines.

Water ordeal. A person would be tied up to be unable to swim and then thrown into the river. If the person sank and drowned she was innocent, otherwise she was burned at the stake.

Witch Trials

"The way to see by faith is to shut the eye of reason."
- Benjamin Franklin:

North Berwick witch trials (1590-1592)

These trials occurred in Berwick, Scotland. About a hundred witches were arrested and confessed under torture to meetings at the church with the Devil where they devoted themselves to doing evil doings. They also confessed to poisoning the King and members of the royal palace, and trying to sink the King's ship.

Agnes Sampson was singled out by James VI. Fastened to the wall of her cell with an iron instrument forced into the mouth so that two prongs pressed against the tongue, and another two prongs pressed against her cheeks. Held in this position with a rope around her neck she was kept without sleep. Agnes Sampson in the end confessed to fifty-three indictments against her. She was finally strangled and burned as a witch.

Fulda (Germany) witch trials (1603-1606)

Prince Bishop Balthasar von Dernbach ordered a witch hunt which resulted in about two hundred people being persecuted and killed.

Würzburg witch trial (1626-1631)

"In August, 1629, the Chancellor of the Prince-Bishop of Würzburg wrote:[32]

"As to the affair of the witches, which Your Grace thinks brought to an end before this, it has started up afresh, and no words can do justice to it. Ah, the woe and the misery of it--there are still four hundred in the city, high and low, of every rank and sex, nay, even clerics, so strongly accused that they may be arrested at any hour. It is true that, of the people of my Gracious Prince here, some out of all offices and faculties must be executed: clerics, electoral councilors and doctors, city officials, court assessors, several of whom Your Grace knows. There are law students to be arrested. The Prince-Bishop has over forty students who are soon to be pastors; among them thirteen or fourteen are said to be witches. A few days ago a Dean was arrested; two others who were summoned have fled. The notary of our Church consistory, a very learned man, was yesterday arrested and put to the torture. In a word, a third part of the city is surely involved. The richest, most attractive, most prominent, of the clergy are already executed. A week ago a maiden of nineteen was executed, of whom it is everywhere said that she was

---

[32] "The original Sources of European History. Vol III" edited by George L Burr. 1896

the fairest in the whole city, and was held by everybody a girl of singular modesty and purity. She will be followed by seven or eight others of the best and most attractive persons. . . . And thus many are put to death for renouncing God and being at the witch-dances, against whom nobody has ever else spoken a word. To conclude this wretched matter, there are children of three and four years, to the number of three hundred, who are said to have had intercourse with the Devil. I have seen put to death children of seven, promising students of the age of ten, twelve, fourteen, and fifteen. Of the nobles--but I cannot and must not write more of this misery. There are persons of yet higher rank, whom you know, and would marvel to hear of, nay, would scarcely believe it; let justice be done . . .

P. S.--Though there are many wonderful and terrible things happening, it is beyond doubt that, at a place called the Fraw-Rengberg, the Devil in person, with eight thousand of his followers, held an assembly and celebrated mass before them all, administering to his audience (that is, the witches) turnip-rinds and parings in place of the Holy Eucharist. There took place not only foul but most horrible and hideous blasphemies, whereof I shudder to write. It is also true that they all vowed not to be enrolled in the Book of Life, but all agreed to be inscribed by a notary who is well known to me and my colleagues. We hope, too, that the book in which they are enrolled will yet be found, and there is no little search being made for it."

Initially the Cologne City Fathers were lenient, but under pressure from the Prince-archbishop in 1627 the city began to impose harsher measures. Persecution raged most violently in Bonn, the Prince-archbishop's own capital. On his authority, his wife and the archbishop's secretary's wife were executed. Even children of three and four years were accused as well as students and small boys of noble birth were sent to the bonfire.

People Burned:-

- Three play-actors.
- Four innkeepers.
- Three common councilmen of Würzburg.
- Fourteen vicars of the Cathedral.
- The burgomaster's lady (wife of the mayor).
- The apothecar's wife and daughter.
- Two choristers of the cathedral.
- Gobel Babelin, The prettiest girl in town.
- The wife, the two little sons and the daughter of councillor Stolzenberg.
- Baunach, The fattest burgher (merchant) in Wurzburg.
- Steinacher, The richest burgher in Wurzburg.
- A wandering boy, twelve years of age.
- Four strange men and women, found sleeping in the market-place.

- A little maiden nine years of age.
- A maiden still less than nine.
- Her little sister, their mother and their aunt.
- A pretty young woman of twenty-four.
- Two boys of twelve.
- A girl of fifteen.
- The young heir of the house of Rotenhahn, aged nine.
- A boy of ten.
- A boy, twelve years old.

Bamberg witch trials (1626-1631)

Took place in Bamberg in Germany in 1626–1631 and are among the more famous cases in European witchcraft history. They resulted in the executions of between 300 and 600 people, and were some of the biggest witch trials in history, as well as some of the most infamous executions in the Thirty Years War.

The Prince-bishop of Bamberg built a witch-house, complete with torture-chamber adorned with appropriate biblical texts.

The bishop's chancellor, Dr. Haan, was burnt for showing 'suspicious leniency' as a judge. Under torture he confessed to having seen five burgomasters (town councillors) of Bamberg at a sabbat (pagan ritual), and they too were duly burnt: one of them was Johannes Junius, whose testimony follows.

A letter in a shaky hand is preserved in Bamberg, secretly written by Johannes Junius to his daughter while in the midst of his trial (July 24, 1628):[33]

"Many hundred thousand good-nights, my dearly beloved daughter Veronica.
Innocent have I come into prison, innocent have I been tortured, innocent must I die. For whoever comes into the witch prison must become a witch or be tortured until he invents something out of his head and--God pity him--bethinks him of something. I will tell you how it has gone with me. When I was the first time put to the torture, Dr. Braun, Dr. Kotzendorffer, and two strange doctors were there. Then Dr. Braun asks me, "Kinsman, how come you here?" I answer, "Through falsehood, through misfortune." "Hear, you," he says, "you are a witch; will you confess it voluntarily? If not, we'll bring in witnesses and the executioner for you." I said "I am no witch, I have a pure conscience in the matter; if there are a thousand witnesses, I am not anxious, but I'll gladly hear the witnesses." Now the chancellor's son

---

[33] Translated by George L. Burr-1896 – "The Witch Persecutions"

was set before me . . . and afterward Hoppfen Elss. She had seen me dance on Haupts-moor. . . . I answered: "I have never renounced God, and will never do it--God graciously keep me from it. I'll rather bear whatever I must." And then came also--God in highest Heaven have mercy--the executioner, and put the thumb-screws on me, both hands bound together, so that the blood ran out at the nails and everywhere, so that for four weeks I could not use my hands, as you can see from the writing. . . . Thereafter they first stripped me, bound my hands behind me, and drew me up in the torture. Then I thought heaven and earth were at an end; eight times did they draw me up and let me fall again, so that I suffered terrible agony. . . .

And this happened on Friday, June 30, and with God's help I had to bear the torture. . . . When at last the executioner led me back into the prison, he said to me: "Sir, I beg you, for God's sake confess something, whether it be true or not. Invent something, for you cannot endure the torture which you will be put to; and, even if you bear it all, yet you will not escape, not even if you were an earl, but one torture will follow after another until you say you are a witch. Not before that," he said, "will they let you go, as you may see by all their trials, for one is just like another." . . .

And so I begged, since I was in wretched plight, to be given one day for thought and a priest. The priest was refused me, but the time for thought was given. Now, my dear child, see in what hazard I stood and still stand. I must say that I am a witch, though I am not, --must now renounce God, though I have never done it before. Day and night I was deeply troubled, but at last there came to me a new idea. I would not be anxious, but, since I had been given no priest with whom I could take counsel, I would myself think of something and say it. It were surely better that I just say it with mouth and words, even though I had not really done it; and afterwards I would confess it to the priest, and let those answer for it who compel me to do it. . . . And so I made my confession, as follows; but it was all a lie.

Now follows, dear child, what I confessed in order to escape the great anguish and bitter torture, which it was impossible for me longer to bear."

Torsåker witch trials

These took place in 1675 in Torsåker parish, Sweden and were the largest witch trial in Sweden.

The priest made two boys stand at the church door to identify "witches" by an "invisible mark" on their forehead. One of these boys pointed at the wife of the priest, to the outrage of the people. She later told her grandson that she had slapped the boy who quickly apologized when he realised who she was, saying he had been blinded by the sun.

Friends and families of the accused were forced to lead, 71 people, 65 women and six men, to their place of execution.

The witch-hunt in the country continued and reached the capital, where it lasted until 1676, ending with the execution of Malin Matsdotter in Stockholm. Authorities then proved that the child witnesses were lying. In 1677, all priests in the country were ordered to tell their congregations that the witches had been expelled forever. In Torsåker, the boys who had pointed out the 'witches' were found with their throats cut.

Trier witch trials (1581-1587)

The persecutions started in the diocese of Trier in 1581 and reached the city itself in 1587. Here it led to the death of 360 people within the city itself, but the numbers of executed was even larger outside of the city. The total number executed is estimated at about a thousand, the biggest mass-execution in Europe outside of war.

People, irrespective of gender, ages or status were victims. In twenty-two villages, between 1587 and 1593, 368 people were burned alive for sorcery. In 1588 in two villages, all people were killed except one female in each village.

People who supported the Inquisitors in their task grew rich. The goods of the executed were confiscated and the children banished. The executioner, whose horse was stained with blood, rode it like a nobleman, dressed in gold and silver and his wife flashed wealth like a lady of the court.

When pestilence invaded the territory of Trier, farming ceased. The resulting famine and deteriorating circumstances were further blamed on witches. The Inquisition and persecution became ruthless and knew no bounds. There was often doubt about the guilt of many. This persecution lasted for several years, some of those who presided over the administration of 'justice' glorified themselves by the many stakes on which human beings had been burned alive.

The classical period of witch-hunts in Europe occurred around 1480 to 1700, straddling the upheavals of the Reformation and resulting in about 40,000 to 100,000 executions, mostly involving burning at the stake.

Salem witch trials (1692)

This episode is one of many infamous cases of mass hysteria, and has been used in political rhetoric and popular literature as a vivid example of the dangers of isolationism, religious extremism, superstition, false accusations and lapses in due process.

Fourteen women and five men were executed by hanging in Salem, Massachusetts, USA. One man, Giles Corey, refused to enter a plea and was crushed to death under heavy stones in an attempt to force him to do so. At least five more of the accused died in prison.

Torture of Children

The Inquisitor Jean Bodin (1529-96), author of "De La Demonomanie des Sorciers" (The Demono-mania of Witches), preferred children as witnesses to extract confessions because they were easily persuaded to confess. The treatment of witches' children was particularly brutal.

Estimates of Witches Executed

Ronald Hutton, in "Counting the Witch Hunt", estimated 40,000 witch executions. Brian Levack (*The Witch Hunt in Early Modern Europe*) increased the number to 60,000 by multiplying the average executions by the number of witch trials.

Whatever number one wishes to believe, what matters here is the gross brutality that pervaded these atrocities, its infrastructure and the moral framework created, using religion.

"And about the ninth hour Jesus cried out with a loud voice, saying, Eli, *Eli, lema sabachthani?*, (My God, my God, why have you forsaken me?)"

~Mathew 27:46

Beyond the Dark Ages

There comes a time to face reality. Elements of absolutism are present in all authoritarian organizations such as Christianity, Islam, Hitler's Germany, Stalin's Russia and Pol Pot's Cambodia and in many new-age religions, such as Jim Jones' People's Temple and Aum Shinrikyo, to name but a few. Atrocities like those of the Dark Ages are strewn across history, justified and modelled on religious absolutism.

Here are examples of atrocities influenced by absolutism:

Nazi Holocaust

This is an example of early childhood gestalts forming the foundation of personality and beliefs as an adult. We refer to the chapter "Personal Ecology".

In his book "Mein Kampf" Hitler praises the Abbot of the monastery in his hometown in Northern Austria who supplemented his schooling in high school. Hitler was strongly influenced by the Abbot's rhetorical skills. Later, as Chancellor of Germany, often referred to God in his public addresses, frequently visited and was proudly photographed with the German Archbishop.

Kristallnacht: The November 1938 Pogroms

During the night of 9 to 10 November, 1938, encouraged by the Nazi regime, anti-Jewish mobs plundered and destroyed synagogues, Jewish-owned stores, hospitals, schools, community centres, cemeteries, and homes. Rioters destroyed nearly 300 synagogues and vandalized or looted Jewish businesses. At least 91 Jewish people were killed. Police and emergency services remained passive. Known as "Kristallnacht", this pogrom led to the intensification of anti-Semite sentiment that peaked in the Holocaust. Leading up to these events, Hitler said:

> "I believe today that I am acting according to the sentiments of the Almighty Creator: By warding off the Jew I am fighting for the Lord's work"
> ~ Adolf Hitler [34]

The Nazi regime was characterized by huge rallies, similar to religious events, where Hitler was hailed as an all-powerful leader and saluted with "Heil Hitler" amid great pomp and ceremony. Speeches were characterised by emotional rhetoric, emphasising the superiority of the German folk.

---

[34] Adolf Hitler "Mein Kampf". Translation- REYNAL & HITCHCOCK- NEW YORK 1941

Estimates of the WWII genocide in Germany are in the region of 6 to 9 million, peaking more than two thousand years of religious persecution against Jews.

Gulag Archipelago

Joseph Stalin was educated in a Christian School in Gori, Georgia, Russia. A good scholar, he received a bursary to study in the Georgian Orthodox Seminary of Tiflis in preparation for priesthood.

As the leader of the Soviet Union, he resurrected the Russian Orthodox Church which had been previously persecuted, but continued persecution of all other religious denominations. Many thousands of priests, monks and nuns of non-Russian Orthodox denominations were killed during these persecutions.

His rallies were often a show of military strength. He, of course, took centre stage.

Joseph Stalin launched, what became known by several authors as "The Soviet Holocaust", the equivalent of the Spanish Inquisition. It involved purges of his (Communist) Party, repression of peasants, deportations of ethnic minorities, and the persecution of unaffiliated persons. The regime was characterized by widespread police surveillance. Suspicious "saboteurs" were imprisoned or murdered. Estimates of the number of people who perished during his rule are as high as 30 million.

Khmer Rouge

Pol Pot (1925 – 1998), real name Saloth Sar, in 1935 attended the École Miche, a Catholic school in Phnom Penh. He was a Cambodian Communist revolutionary, leading the Khmer Rouge from 1963 until his death in 1998. After seizing power, April 17, 1975, he ruled Cambodia as despotic dictator.

His policy of agrarian socialism forced urban dwellers to relocate to the countryside and work on collective farms in a forced labour system. A combination of executions, exhaustion, malnutrition, and poor medical care resulted in the deaths of approximately 25 percent of the Cambodian population. [35]

Hundreds of thousands of people, mainly the educated, who had relocated from the cities were caught and forced to dig their own mass graves. They were then buried alive by Khmer Rouge soldiers. "Bullets are not to be wasted." These mass graves are referred to as "The Killing Fields".

Although methods differed from the Inquisitions, the diseased mindset of authoritarianism was the same.

---

[35] Craig Etcheson - *After the Killing Fields*

Some 20,000 grave sites were found containing the remains of 1,386,734 victims. UNICEF estimated that 3 million had been killed.

Rwanda

In Rwanda, two nuns and a priest were convicted for their part in the genocide that massacred 800 000 people.

Bosnia

July 1995: an estimated 8,000 Bosnian men and boys were murdered in the region of Srebrenica in Bosnia and Herzegovina by units of the Army of Republika Srpska, an Orthodox group.

Anti-abortionists

Women's health clinics that provide abortions have been targets of violence. Religious terrorists and terrorist organizations include the Army of God, The Lambs of Christ, Clayton Waagner, Mike Bray, James Kopp, Paul Jennings Hill and Eric Robert Rudolph.

Evangelical Protestants

Southern United States evangelical Protestants, in the late nineteenth century, used a wide range of terror tactics, including lynching, murder, attempted murder, rape, beating, tar-and-feathering, whipping, and destruction of property, to suppress competition from Mormons, Jews, Catholics and black Christians.

The Peoples Temple

The "People's Temple" was organized and founded in 1955 by Jim Jones, who led 918 people to their mass suicide on November 18, 1978 in Guyana by means of "Armageddon" (End of the World) preaching.

Islamist Extremism

After Muhammad's death a number of wars broke out as militants sought to take control of Islam. No war was decisive in producing one leader; instead different leaders established Caliphates that controlled some variations of Islam in a number of regions.

The power balance of these Caliphates protected Arabia from an equivalent "Dark Age" in Islam. However, the elements of extremism are alive in many Islamist organisations, such as Al Qaeda and its off-shoots such as Boko Haram.

Before 20th century globalisation, Western culture had a limited influence on Islam. When a Western coalition force from 34 nations, led by the United States, acted against Iraq in response to its invasion and annexation of Kuwait, anxiety took on religious proportions. Extremists, like al-Qaeda, took this opportunity to wage a holy war.

Lacking the military resources of the West, their weapon was suicide.

Attempts at profiling terrorist personalities are unsuccessful. The consensus among psychologists, political scientists and sociologists was that terrorists are not diagnosable as mentally sick people. **The differentiating element, Religion, is overlooked.**

"There seems to be general agreement among psychologists that there is no particular psychological attribute that can be used to describe the terrorist." [36]

"None of the suicide bombers (they ranged in age from eighteen to thirty one) conformed to the typical profile of the suicidal personality. None of them were uneducated, desperately poor, simple-minded, or depressed. Many were middle class and, unless they were fugitive, had paying jobs. More than half of them were refugees from what is now Israel. Two were the sons of millionaires. They all seemed to be normal members of their families. They were polite and serious; and in their communities they were considered to be [36] - Hudson report "The sociology and Psychology of Terrorism: who becomes a terrorist and why?" - September 1999. Federal Research Division Library of Congress model youths. Most were bearded.

All were deeply religious."

- Riaz Hassan, 2001- Global Rise of Suicide Terrorism: An Overview. - Asian Journal of Social Science 36 (2008) 271-291

———

"Love of martyrdom is something deep inside (.the religious heart.), but these rewards are not in themselves the goal of the martyr. The only aim is to win Allah's satisfaction. That can be done in the simplest and speediest of manner by dying in the cause of Allah. And it is Allah who selects martyrs".

- Sheikh Yassin

Al Qaeda

In 1992, the first attack by Al Qaeda was carried out in Aden, targeting American troops staying at the Gold Mohur hotel, and a second bomb at the Aden Movenpick which detonated prematurely, killing two Australian tourists. Osama Bin Laden later claimed responsibility for these attacks.

In February 1993 Ramzi Yousef parked a van full of explosives in the garage beneath the World Trade Center. The explosion claimed six victims and over a thousand were wounded. Ramzi Yousef, was the nephew of Khalid Sheikh Mohammed, who planned the 9/11 attacks.

In October 2000 Al Qaeda succeeded in a suicide attack on the United States Naval vessel, USS Cole, anchored in a Yemeni port for routine refuelling.

September 11, 2001: al-Qaeda terrorists hijacked four commercial airliners, their passengers and crew. Two flew into the World Trade Centre buildings and destroyed them, one into the Pentagon and one crashed near Shanksville, Pennsylvania, as passengers and crew frustrated the attempt by the terrorists to ram the airliner into Capitol Hill in Washington. 2,974 innocent people were maliciously murdered that day.

12 October 2002, in the popular tourist district of Kuta on the Indonesian island of Bali, three simultaneous attacks by members of Jemaah Islamiyah, a violent Islamist group, detonated a car bomb near a popular nightclub, a suicide bomber carried a backpack and a third bomb was detonated outside the United States consulate in Denspasar. 202 innocent people were murdered and 240 were injured.

November, 2003, suicide bombers drove two trucks into the Bet Israel and Neve Shalom synagogues in Istanbul, Turkey. This devastated the synagogues. Of the innocent people who died, 21 were Turkish Muslims and 6 were Jews. More than 300 were injured. An Islamic militant group The Great Eastern Islamic Raiders' Front claimed responsibility.

February 27, 2004, Islamic terrorists placed a bomb in the most crowded part of the ferry Super-Ferry 14 and caused the deaths of 116 people in the Philippines, among them six children less than five years old, nine children between six and 16 years of age and six students.

11 March 2004, three days before the Spanish election, the Madrid commuter train system was bombed 911 days after the 9/11 events. During the peak of the Madrid morning rush hour a number of explosions occurred aboard four commuter trains. As of 11 April 2006, 29 suspects were charged for their involvement in theses train bombings. 191 innocent people were murdered.

29 May 2004: seventeen terrorists, members of the Jerusalem Squadron (a militant Islamist organization), attacked a foreign workers compound in Al-Khobar, Saudi Arabia. During the siege 41 hostages were freed, 25 were injured and 22 were murdered. 14 attackers were killed and 3 escaped.

July 7, 2005: Three Pakistani's of British descent and a British Jamaican attacked London's public transport system by detonating three bombs in the London Underground and one on a double decker bus. 56 innocent people died and about 700 were injured.

179

17 November 1997: Al-Gama'a al-Islamiyya, the Egyptian Islamist organization, murdered 62 people, mostly innocent tourists, at Deir el-Bahri, an archaeological site near Luxor.

July 23, 2005: an Islamist group executed a series of terror attacks on the Egyptian resort city of Sharm el-Sheikh in the southern tip of the Sinai Peninsula.

November 9, 2005. Suicide bombers infiltrated a wedding crowd in the Hayatt Amman Hotel and two other hotels at the same time, murdering 60 innocent people and wounding hundreds.

April 11, 2007 Two bombs exploded simultaneously in Algiers, murdering 33 people. An Al-Qaeda linked organization claimed responsibility.

February 17, 2008. In Kandahar, Afghanistan a crowd of people watching a dog-fighting competition was attacked. More than 100 innocent people died and another 100 injured. The Taliban were suspected.

June 1, 2009, The United States Muslim convert Abdul Hakim Mujahid Muhammad (Carlos Leon Bledsoe) opened fire in a drive-by shooting at a military recruiting office in Little Rock, Arkansas, murdering one US soldier and wounding another. He confessed to being part of Al Queda.

Religious terrorism is an ongoing concern throughout the world. Thousands of innocent people have lost their lives and many more have been wounded, with friends and families suffering lifelong emotional scars.

Other religion-inspired Atrocities

The Lord's Resistance Army is a guerrilla army engaged in an armed rebellion against the Ugandan government, and is accused of many acts of mutilation, torture, rape, abduction, the use of child soldiers and a number of massacres.

The Middle East, the most religious centre of this planet and birthplace of numerous religions, is also one of the most volatile places on this planet.

In Northern Ireland, for decades innocent people, enjoying time with family and friends, were murdered by bombs, leaving children orphaned, blinded or their limbs broken and ripped from their bodies.

In Nigeria, 12000 people have died in clashes between Christian and Muslim tribes since 1999.

Iraq. In 2005, there were 400 incidents of suicide bombing, killing more than 2000 people - most of them innocent civilians. In 2006, almost half of all reported terrorist attacks in the world (6600), and more than half of all terrorist fatalities (13,000) occurred in Iraq.

181

Analysis

"Man's loathsome cruelty to man is his most outstanding characteristic; it is explicable only in terms of his carnivorous and cannibalistic origin. Robert Hartmann (1832 - 1893 German naturalist, anatomist and ethnographer) pointed out that 'both rude and civilised people show unspeakable cruelty to one another. We call it inhuman cruelty; but these dreadful things are unhappily truly human, because there is nothing like them in the animal world.'"
— Raymond A. Dart - Africa's Place in the Emergence of Civilisation (1959)

Creationists probably find it difficult to understanding this analysis and therefore cannot find effective solutions. This we noticed from the turgid reaction of the Catholic Church, in response to allegations of sexual predation of children. We also note similar reluctance among Islam clergy in condemning abuse of women and "honour killings". Typical of predator behaviour, the weak and defenceless are their victims.

Predation impulses originate from our primate origins, and are responsible for the impulse to dominate the tribe thus ensuring first choice of mate, food and status. The intensity of competitions for dominance should not be underestimated; it often ends in serious injury or death.

The "Domination" gene, expressed through testosterone, produces a better chance of survival. We humans have inherited this domination gene. Extremism is the result of a very human overdrive for power, status and predation.

"An abnormal reaction to an abnormal situation is normal behavior."
— Viktor E. Frankl, Man's Search for Meaning

The following scientific studies examine the nature of unchecked alpha domination.

Influence of Authority

"Blind belief in authority is the greatest enemy of truth"
- Albert Einstein

"Those who can make you believe in absurdities can make you commit atrocities'."
~Voltaire

Psychologist Stanley Milgram, curious about the motives of Nazi war criminals, designed an experiment to establish if normal, healthy individuals would follow instructions, given by an authority figure, even though it meant harmful or even deadly consequences for another person.

Volunteers were assigned the task of "teaching" word associations. Unknown to the volunteer was that the "learner", behind a closed door, was a collaborator, communicating through a microphone system.

The volunteer was told to administer an electric shock to the "learner" when he made a mistake. The unseen learner was not connected to any shock equipment, but recorded sound effects, expressing pain, were piped to the volunteer.

The volunteer's task was to increase the voltage each time the "learner" made a mistake. The sound effects reflected increasing pain. The maximum shock voltage on the volunteer's instrument indicated 450 volts, enough to kill a person.

The key to this experiment is that an authoritative looking person would confirm the reality of the "learner's responses" but encouraged the volunteer to continue increasing the voltage, even when the voltage appeared to get dangerously high and the learner's response indicated agony, pain and possible death.

A survey, held before the experiment, indicated that most people believed that only 1.2% of volunteers would apply the maximum voltage. In reality, the study showed that 65% of volunteers applied the maximum, 450 volts.

"Ordinary people, simply doing their jobs, without any particular hostility on their part, can become agents in a terrible destructive process. Moreover, even when the destructive effects of their work become patently clear and they are asked to carry out actions incompatible with fundamental standards of morality, relatively few people have the resources needed to resist authority."
-Stanley Milgram (1974). - The Perils of Obedience.

The "Lucifer Effect"

A study, by Prof Philip Zimbardo in the early 1960's, sheds light on the psychology of ordinary people when given unchecked dominance over others. The results of this study were unexpected.[37]

A mock prison was set up at Stanford University and 24 mentally healthy students were chosen. By random selection, 12 were "Guards" and 12 were "Prisoners". Everyones' identity was obscured; "Guards" wore uniforms and dark glasses to symbolise authority and "Prisoners" wore a simple smock and head cover. "Prisoners" were addressed by their numbers only.

---

[37] Philip Zimbardo- "The Lucifer Effect"

The intention was to run the study for two weeks but it was terminated *only after six days,* when "Guards" became abusive and sadistic in subjugating the "Prisoners". Arbitrary humiliating rituals were invented by the "Guards" to subjugate the "Prisoners", who already showed signs of stress. The speed, with which abuse started, caught many off guard, including Dr Zimbardo.

Dr Zimbardo found parallels of this experiment with the mistreatment of prisoners by military personnel at Abu Ghraib during the Afghan War. There, abuses were committed from late 2003 to early 2004, in the form of physical, psychological, and sexual abuse, including torture, rape, sodomy, and homicide.

Extreme domination arises in an ecology of beliefs of supremacy, coupled with overwhelming control of one group over another. The process begins with de-individuation, de-humanization, victimisation and moral disengagement by the dominant group, triggering the Predator Instinct.

> "Any deed that any human being has ever committed, however horrible, is possible for any of us – under the right or wrong situational circumstances."
> ~The Lucifer Effect - Dr. Philip Zimbardo

Religious Domination

In the light of the above studies, we examine the part religion plays in atrocities.

Organised Religion is a powerful instrument for social engineering. Any individual or institution that convincingly argues that they are an *intercessor* of an *invisible*, all-powerful, all-knowing, omnipresent God conjures up overwhelming influence.

Social engineering in antiquity grew from a desire, of the ruling elite, to control expanding human communities. Christianity and Islam designed their dogmas to boost their authoritarianism. Rules become moral principles, embedded by dramatic rhetoric and regular ritual activity.

When Constantine faced the problems of the huge, fragile Roman Empire, he saw religion as a solution. Placing himself at the head of all religions, which included all pagan religions, he drew attention to himself as both a religious and a secular leader. This, he envisaged, would to reduce disunity in the Empire. His example was not a novel idea; rulers, such as Pharaohs, Emperors, Kings and Muslim Caliphs manipulated religions to propagate their supposed divine powers.

Gradually religious institutions commandeered the social engineering process and transformed it into absolute

187

domination behind the cloak of Heresy, Blasphemy and Apostasy.

Institutional Terror

Absolute Fear

Closer relationship of Barons with ordinary people in the fiefdoms gave ordinary people more influence. The Barons understood and communicated the activities in the fiefdoms to the emperor. This reduced the need for social engineering. The Emperor had less need for the Church to support his authority. This resulted in the downgrade of the papacy in the hierarchy of imperial needs. Popes could no longer rely on Emperors and the ruling elite to influence behaviour.

The Church was losing influence, doctrine and direction. God was no help either. The Church faced a growing fear of its uncertain existence. This threat developed into an existential anxiety and a struggle for its survival ensued.

The events of the Dark Ages were a long time in the making. The inability of the Christian Churches to agree on theological issues at the Nicaea Council and Constantine's determination to unify the Christian Churches meant that some variations had to be excluded and labelled 'Heretic'. The early struggle that ensued resulted in the murder of 10 000 Origenist monks as well as Hypatia, the influential female head of the Platonist school at Alexandria.

Christian unity, originally enforced by Constantine, crumbled as variations of Christianity reappeared in various forms such as the Cathars, Waldensians and Arians. In addition, Muslim Caliphates were battering at the doors of Christian Europe.

Phobia

Religious beliefs are based on paradigms superstitions. Both are emotive fantasies, based on meagre anecdotal evidence and skimpy analysis. Thus, religious people are easily persuaded to respond to fantasy as if reality.

Adding to the general anxiety of the Church were the phobias of citizens. These beliefs resulted from the animated rhetoric of sermons motivating Inquisitions and Witch Hunts. Persistent threats (real or imagined) lead to unhealthy physical and mental stress responses, which affect the immune system, stimulates psychoses, depression and unusual behaviour. This unusual behaviour then further justified fantasies of Witches and Satan.

Witches

- The mythology of witches was exacerbated by religious assertions that phenomena of diseases, such as the plague, cholera, measles, mumps found in crowded towns, were the doings of evil spirits. In addition chaos, caused by bad weather, crop failures and animal deaths led to increasing negative effects on towns-people. Scientific explanations had, of course, not yet reached the minds of ordinary people and superstition filled the vacuum of knowledge. Witchcraft was a simple way to explain the inability of God to end the misery of even the most pious people.

Satan

- Gifted people were targeted for allegedly making pacts with the devil in return for their special gifts or wealth. These were a favoured target of Inquisitors, who seized the assets of these victims to enrich themselves and the church.
- Still preached in the 21st century is the idea that bad feelings are the result of the devil's work.

Heaven and Hell

- The threat of everlasting heaven or hell is a simple "Carrot and Stick" motivation strategy that works on the superstitious. Authoritative knowledge of the afterlife is only available to the dead.

Absolute Superiority

The first step to institutional domination is a declaration of self-proclaimed sacred authority. This is to ward off challenges to the decrees of the dictatorship or religion. To assuage possible discomfort by the subjugated, people are indoctrinated to believe that their affiliation to such elitist group is assured, provided they follow the doctrine.

> **2 Corinthians 6:14** - Be ye not unequally yoked together with unbelievers: for what fellowship hath righteousness with unrighteousness? and what communion hath light with darkness?

Absolute Intolerance

Tenets of Heresy, Blasphemy and Apostasy, common to Christianity and Islam, are designed to protect their dogma from critical evaluation. Transgressors of these tenets are condemned to everlasting hell.

These tenets hide the existential fear of religious institutions when confronted by contesting ideas. Therefore, according to the absolute mind, naysayers must be eliminated from the debate by any means possible, including the use of crimes against humanity, genocide, torture, public humiliation and a tortuous death.

191

Absolute Subjugation

In a state of ignorance, it is natural to refer to an authority for guidance. Sadly, for the victims of the Dark Ages, the credentials of the ultimate authority, God, comes via individuals who have their own agenda.

Humility and submission, as a virtue, is a pervasive theme. Religious literature and sermons constantly emphasise humility and obedience.

> Romans 13: 1, 2, 5
> "¹ Let everyone be subject to the governing authorities, for there is no authority except that which God has established. The authorities that exist have been established by God.
> ² Consequently, whoever rebels against the authority is rebelling against what God has instituted, and those who do so will bring judgment on themselves.
> ⁵ Therefore, it is necessary to submit to the authorities, not only because of possible punishment but also as a matter of conscience."

"Islam" means submission and obedience to God. Muslims submit or surrender to God, recognizing Muhammad as God's prophet. According to Muslim theology, mankind's chief failing is pride and rebellion. In their pride, humans attempt to partner themselves with

God and thereby damage the authority of God. Thus, pride is Islam's cardinal sin. The cardinal virtue, then, is submission, or *Islam*.

We have shown that it is the nature of humankind to challenge and compete. It is healthy when it establishes a balance of power. We know, from history, how disastrous authoritarian institutions are. In a *democracy*, the "rulers" are regarded as servants, and the *people* are the real rulers.

Absolute Virtue

The Church's belief in its own perfection and virtue is validated by its own, absolute tenet, that it is the home of an all-mighty, all-wise, and all-powerful God. The Church's doctrine of its infallibility therefore excludes self-analysis. Thus the Church refuses to adapt and proclaims *it* is not at fault but that the problem is evil in others.

Absolute Vilification

During and before the Investiture controversy, many problems beset the Church, not least of which were the many dysfunctional popes and waning support from the nobility. Although the problems stemmed from within the Church, it sought to correct the problem elsewhere, blaming the influence of evil, when it had itself to blame.

Inquisitors, who were at the cutting edge of the Inquisitions and Torture of "Witches", had an extreme perspective of their task. Enforced by dogmas of Heresy, Blasphemy and dramatised rhetoric, which described the victims as inhuman, soulless villains of the devil, Inquisitors perceived the victims with fear and loathing, triggering predatory instincts. The actions of the front-line men were therefore merciless. De-individuation, de-humanization and moral disengagement of Inquisitors led to victimisation, torture, murder and unspeakable atrocities.

This mindset re-appears in the atrocities of the Nazi persecution of Jews, the Soviet Holocaust, the Killing Fields of Cambodia and Charles Manson's "Helter Skelter".

Absolute Loss of Self

There is, with religions, a confusing self-concept. The notion, basic to major religions, is that gods, angels, devils and all manner of mystical beings control behaviour, talents and destinies of men and women. Are we godly, evil or human? Under pressure, this blurred self-concept develops into a befuddled relationship between self and the real world; thus losing robust ownership and responsibility of self and a loss of purpose. This lack of ownership of self drives desperate acts of immorality.

In a study of 65 adults who were incarcerated because of childhood abuse, Dr Abby Stein established the link between dissociated, distorted reasoning of self and adult violence.

She investigated the link between anger, aggression and dissociative states of mind to challenge the view that guilt, fantasy and threat are the cause of violence.[38]

Inquisition decrees by the Papacy ignored their own preaching on morality and transgressed all "Seven Deadly Sins" in an overflowing orgy of terror.

What is a more reliable foundation for morality?

"Millions of innocent men, women, and children, since the introduction of Christianity, have been burned, tortured, fined, and imprisoned, yet we have not advanced one inch toward uniformity. What has been the effect of coercion? To make one half of the world fools and the other half hypocrites"

~Thomas Jefferson

---

[38] Abby Stein - "Prologue to Violence"

Sanity Returns

The Dawn of a New Era

Religious wars cannot be won. They are the ultimate folly. Ideas cannot be forced onto people. Ideas of merit will survive; others expire with the test of reason. An attempt to persist with untested ideas is the very source of folly.

Stalemate

Exhausted by war, combatants recovered their sense of reason and signed the Peace Treaty of Westphalia (May 15 and October 24, 1648). The peace accord saw a shift from attempts to dominate with religious doctrine to the creation of systems that respected boundaries. This was the first modern diplomatic congress to establish order in central Europe based on state sovereignty and became part of the constitutional laws of the Holy Roman Empire and most States thereafter.

The power stalemate leading to the Peace Treaty of Westphalia also ended the worst Dark Age horrors. Absolutism cannot exist where there is a balance of power.

The above is also true for Islam. Immediately after the death of Muhammad, the conflict for control of Islam ended in a stalemate, ending a period of civil wars and saved the region from another "Dark Age".

Today, pockets of Islamic absolutism exist in a number of regions. Pakistan, Iran, Saudi Arabia, Africa and Afghanistan comes to mind. Here absolutism leads to the subjugation of women, witch-phobia and religion motivated wars.

Resilience of Ideas.

Intolerance to new ideas will limit the development of realistic beliefs that synchronise with reality. Absolute intolerance closes the mind. Like a dead branch, the intolerant mind will break; despite extreme measures and futile attempts to save it.

An important paradigm shift occurs in an educated mind. Such a mind frees itself from mental slavery through a better understanding of its personal ecology. It develops mental resources to question ideas, concepts, beliefs and methods.

We see thus a gradual shift after the implementation of Charlemagne's educational system. First, the middle class, then slaves themselves, rejected the idea of enslavement. This process led, eventually, to the development of democratic systems, where the "rulers" become the servants and the citizen is king. This arrangement fundamentally clashes with the elements of absolutism in religion and autocratic governments.

The shift to democracy produces a better, more prosperous and safer society.

The Reformation

The Christian Reformation

The ongoing corruption, abuse and dereliction of the papal office from the 9th Century eventually led to the Protestant Reformation. It started in 1517 whith the "Ninety-Five Theses" posted on a church door in Germany by Martin Luther. It protested clerical abuses, in particular the sale of indulgences in remission of sins. John Calvin, Huldrych Zwingli and others also played important roles during the Reformation and the rise of Protestant Churches. The invention of the printing press enabled wide-spread announcement of grievances and reasons for the creation of Protestantism.

Wars of religion continued through the sixteenth and seventeenth Centuries. The Thirty Years' War (1618–1648) was initially fought as a religious conflict between Protestants and Catholics in the Holy Roman Empire. It inevitably degenerated into wars of revenge and retribution and prolonged it beyond reason, similar to the Northern Ireland conflict in the 19-20th Century. The impact of the war was the extensive destruction of the entire region. Foraging armies denuded plains and grasslands. Episodes of famine and disease decimated the population of central Europe and bankrupted the combatants.

Renaissance and Humanism

The European wars of religion, fought mainly in the German and Frankish regions, left Italy in a state of relative peace. This region gave rebirth to human creativity and inventiveness. The cultural movement of the Renaissance began in Florence and spanned roughly the 14th to the 17th century into the late medieval age, spreading to the rest of Europe.

The development of the printing press allowed the rapid transmission of new ideas. Its effect was to spread, diversify and change culture.

The Renaissance is a testimony to the resilience of humanity and its resistance to the psychotic obsession to control mind, body and person. The Humanist philosophies, based on the love and dignity of humanity, embody the concept that humans are inherently good and have an inborn capacity to free themselves.

The father of Humanism, Petrarch (1304-1374), well-known for his break from traditional thinking and a new emphasis on learning and creativity. Leonardo Bruni (1369-1444), was first to use the word umanista (Humanism), to emphasize the importance of humankind. This began the development of secular beliefs within society.

People of the Renaissance

Artists

Leonardo da Vinci - Leonardo di serPiero da Vinci (1452 – 1519) was an Italian scientist, mathematician, engineer, inventor, anatomist, painter, sculptor, architect, botanist, musician and writer. Leonardo da Vinci has often been described as the archetype of the Renaissance man, a man whose unquenchable curiosity was equalled only by his powers of invention. He is widely considered to be one of the greatest painters of all time and perhaps the most diversely talented person to have ever lived.

John Milton (1608 – 1674) was an English poet, author and civil servant for the British Commonwealth. He is best known for his epic poem "Paradise Lost" and for his stand against censorship.

William Shakespeare (1564 – 1616) the English poet and playwright, is widely regarded as the greatest writer in the English language and the world's greatest dramatist.

Michelangelo - Michelangelo di Lodovico Buonarroti Simoni (1475 – 1564) A prolific painter, sculptor, architect, poet, and engineer, famous for his paintings on the Sistine Chapel ceiling, the statue of David, the statue of Moses, Madonna of Bruges, the *Pietà* (Jesus on the lap of his mother Mary) and many other profoundly moving works of art.

Scientists

Nicolaus Copernicus (1473 −1543) was the first astronomer to formulate a comprehensive sun-centred (heliocentric) cosmology, which displaced the Earth from the centre of the universe. His book, *De revolutionibus orbium coelestium* (On the Revolutions of the Celestial Spheres), published in 1543 just before his death, is regarded as the starting point of modern astronomy.

Galileo Galilei (1564 − 1642) the Italian physicist, mathematician, astronomer, and philosopher, played a major role in the Scientific Revolution. His achievements include improvements to the telescope and the consequent astronomical observations, and support for Copernicus' helio-centric universe. After 1610, when he supported Copernicus publicly, he met with bitter opposition from some philosophers and clerics. Two clerics eventually denounced him to the Roman Inquisition early in 1615. Although he was cleared of any offence, the Church nevertheless condemned helio-centricism as false and contrary to Scripture in February 1616, and Galileo was warned to abandon the idea. When he again defended his views in his most famous work, "Dialogue Concerning the Two Chief World Systems", published in 1632, the Inquisition tried him, found vehemently suspect of heresy, forced to recant, and spent the rest of his life under house arrest.

Pedro Nunes (1502 - 1578) was a Portuguese mathematician, cosmographer, and professor, born from a New Christian (of Jewish origin) family. Nunes, considered to be one of the greatest mathematicians of his time, is best known for his contributions in the technical field of navigation, which was crucial to the Portuguese period of discoveries.

Francis Bacon (1561 – 1626). His works established and popularised an inductive methodology for scientific inquiry and proposed planned procedures for investigating phenomena.

The Age of Enlightenment

"The Age of Enlightenment broke through the sacred circle whose dogma had circumscribed thinking."
~Peter Gay - The Enlightenment

When Europe recovered from the wars of religion, royal courts flourished. Royals vied for the most beautiful palace architecture, gardens, garments, music, poetry and artworks. Palace entertainment produced new forms of dance, education and refined behaviour.

Overarching the Renaissance from the 17th century, the Age of Enlightenment inspired a Western philosophy advocating reason as the prime source of legitimate understanding and began to break from theological dominance.

Even then, people who challenged religion found this a perilous exercise. Less than 15 years before Hume's birth in 1711, an 18-year-old University student (Thomas Aikenhead) was tried, convicted, and hanged in Edinburgh for blasphemy, saying that Christianity was nonsense.

Idealism

Age of Enlightenment Philosophy often revolved around the issue of Idealism. The whereness of God occupied many of the greatest minds during this period. Does God exist? Where? In an Ideal State?

> Although organised religion insists on the existence of a God, He cannot be detected by the senses such as touch, sight, sound, smell or taste but only through an altered state of consciousness.

Idealism is the philosophical theory that maintains that the nature of reality is based on an ideal, meta-physical state, in contrast to Materialism, which maintains that the nature of reality is based on physical substances.

The philosophical theme of Idealism attempts to define Plato's ideal, mystical state and "Forms". The concept, refined by Plotinus, strongly influenced major religions. As pragmatic paradigms of science evolved, they gradually overshadowed Idealism as follows:

René Descartes (1596 – 1650) asserted that the mind (soul) is as a non-material entity, independent of the laws of physics and only humans have a mind, which interacts with the body through the pineal gland. (Science subsequently discovered that it has nothing to do with a soul but is responsible for the mundane function of regulating wake/sleep patterns)

Bishop George Berkeley (1685 – 1753). Regarded by some as the father of modern idealism, believed that objects depended on our perception for their existence. "esse est percipi:- to be is to be perceived".

Gottfried Wilhelm von Leibniz (1646 – 1716) believed that the criterion of the truth is not sensory but intellectual. All things that humans ordinarily understand as interactions between objects (such as in space and time), have their origin in the mind of God and not in the Universe where we perceive them to be.

Immanuel Kant (1724 –1804) was born into an age of growing scientific influence marked by David Hume, Johannes Kepler, Galileo Galilei and Isaac Newton. During this period, the concept "true knowledge is intellectual" was challenged by "true knowledge is observed". Attempting to unify these paradigms, in the "Critique of Pure Reason" he concludes that there are inherent limits to our ability to "know" through philosophical reasoning. "We experience only appearances, not things in themselves". This work created a significant paradigm shift in philosophical debates and reflected the gradual loosening of the grip of religious ideas over philosophy.

Idealism offered no benefit in developing practical solutions. Scientific and engineering principles grew and underpinned the development of the Industrial Revolution.

Friedrich Nietzsche (1844 –1900) Nietzsche believed that we must transform ourselves into exemplary human beings by crafting our own identity and achieve the "über-mensch" (transformed human) instead of relying on transcendence into a mystical, spiritual being. Nietzsche believed human actions are motivated by the desire to develop one's self.

Alfred Korzybski. (1879 –1950) The map is not the territory! - Polish-American scientist and philosopher, encapsulating his view that abstraction derived from something, or a reaction to it, is not the real thing.

> We were reminded of a children's party some time ago. The children were called onto the lawn and told that whoever caught the bright blue balloon would win a prize. The balloon was thrown into the air and as it drifted down the children jumped to catch it. Bumping against one another, they only managed to bounce it back into the air. Eventually, a few of them managed to grab the balloon simultaneously; the balloon popped and vanished, leaving behind nothing but bewildered children.

Separating Fact from Fiction

"I had to deny knowledge in order to make room for faith."
— Immanuel Kant, Critique of Pure Reason

As the brain evolved, humankind began to understand the dynamics of its ecology. This understanding is necessary for planning, to prevent disaster, improve security and increase pleasure.

One way of improving understanding is by comparison using similes, metaphors or allegories. In this way we use our imagination to speculate about our personal ecology. For instance, we can imagine lightning to be like a discharge of electricity, similar to the spark when electric wires touch each other. This analogy was not available to ancient man, so he imagined fictional, humanlike agents, such as Thor as the agent of thunder and lightning.

Ancient humanity, in trying to understand their world, but unable to distinguishing fact from fiction, spontaneously interweaved observation and fantasy to arrive at a faltering understanding of the world. These fantasies evolved into the mythologies that we find in ancient philosophy and religions.

"What then is truth? A movable host of metaphors, metonymies, and anthropomorphisms: in short, a sum of human relations which have been poetically and rhetorically intensified, transferred, and embellished, and which, after long usage, seem to a people to be fixed, canonical, and binding."

~ Friedrich Nietsche ~ Über Wahrheit und Lüge im außermoralischen Sinn

The purpose of scientific methods is to separate fact from speculative notions, thereby establishing a robust basis for realistic understanding.

Reasons for continuing use of mythology

Religious institutions still promote a mythological God as an absolute creator of everything for the following reasons:

1. *When institutions claim to be the sacred authority of mythology, it gives them absolute domination over those who believe in the fantasy. To maintain this delusional authority requires extreme measures, including hypnotic mind control, indoctrination, torture and murder of dissidents.*

209

2. *Believers are indoctrinated into remaining subjects of the institutions, particularly so in Christianity, Islam and Scientology.*

3. *The methodologies of these religions serve as effective instruments for indoctrinating vast populations. Dictators such as Hitler, Stalin, Pol Pot, Jim Jones and many others, used these methods. Evangelists and many religious institutions actively promote these injunctions for their personal power and enrichment.*

Indoctrination Methods

"For those who stubbornly seek freedom around the world, there can be no more urgent task than to come to understand the mechanisms and practices of indoctrination. These are easy to perceive in the totalitarian societies, much less so in the propaganda system to which we are subjected and in which all too often we serve as unwilling or unwitting instruments."[39]

~ Noam Chomsky

Since the beginning of humankind, rhythms of dance, song and chanting (of prayer) produce hypnotic trance.

---

[39] Noam Chomsky "Propaganda, American Style"

This phenomenon puts people into a highly suggestible state. In this trance state, ideas bypass critical reasoning.

Repeated often enough, religious adherents find it difficult to free themselves from unfeasible propositions, despite more rigorous understanding through scientific methods.

This kind of trance is elementary hypnosis and used by therapists to help millions of people worldwide. In the hands of unscrupulous people however, it is used to bypass critical capacities of the mind and open it to irrational ideas and dogmas.

Without the test of rigorous reason, these ideas can mutate into extreme consequences, such as when people beat and kill their own children for "misbehaving".

Cults, Cults and more Cults

There are thousands of cults derived from the two major religions, Islam and Christianity.

One should ask "Why are there so many?" The reason is simple; "it's so easy" because cult leaders model the simple indoctrination methodologies from these religions.

Recruiting methods offer initial comfort and support for people in need. Behind the shop front, however, are all manner of indoctrination techniques imitated from major religions.

New recruits are found among vulnerable people, such as teenage children and those going through difficult times. This is also true for major religions; their methods often involve counselling to addicts and the poor; always with a message to "Return to God". People addicted to drugs are easily addicted to mythology.

Cult leaders are well versed in indoctrination techniques, usually from personal experience as members of religious gatherings. The techniques themselves are easy to copy; all that is required is some oratory skills.

There is very little difference in indoctrination methodologies used by major religions and those by cults; however, Christianity is the grand-daddy of them all.

Who needs Religion?

"The road to hell is paved with good intentions"

Many people seek religion to fill gaps in meaning. Usually these gaps appear in difficult situations, such as personal setbacks, war, relationship issues or moral breakdown in society when terrible things happen to good people.

> "When we are no longer able to change a situation, we are challenged to change ourselves."
> — Viktor E. Frankl, Man's Search for Meaning

There is no doubt that most religious leaders initially have good intentions, but we notice how fragile these intentions become, when driven by a need for dominance.

Consider some intentions of Major Religions:

- **Unifying Mankind.** The intention of Constantine was to unify Christianity; instead, it resulted in a vicious clamouring for power, justified by a belief in Heresy, Blasphemy and Apostasy, which gave Christianity and Islam (following the model of Christianity), a license to kill; the actual kill often "subcontracted" to a secular entity. This set the stage for the Dark Ages.
- Islamic clerics may declare a "Fatwa" (legal

opinion of Sharia law). But it is well known that individuals, driven by religious dogma, take the matter into their own hands, such as parents who kill their children for Apostasy and wives who are stoned for adultery, but men remain exonerated.

- **Providing a Moral Code**. The intention is to provide believers with a useful code of conduct. Instead, religions declare critical phenomena of human nature to be under the control of supernatural influences. They then claim absolute knowledge of the supernatural, only to assert overweening authority and define a self-ingratiating moral code.
- **Developing Compassion**. The intention may have been to develop understanding among people and eliminate conflict, but instead it disembodies control of human behaviour to deities, angels and demons, and confuses the believer as to the true nature of mankind.
- **Demanding Humility and Submission**. The purpose may have been to assure believers that God is attending to their welfare, but instead humility and submission reduces believers to the mentality of slaves, malleable and easy to manipulate.

The behaviour of religious leaders shows all too human character, of Godliness all too little.

The Religion-Free option

Scientific surveys show that Religion-Frees are:

- More Intelligent
- More Compassionate
- Morally more Robust

Intelligence

Intelligence is directly linked to learning activity, such as solving complex problems in mathematics, engineering, medicine, business and science. There is thus a positive correlation between intelligence and facing challenges directly.

Intelligence strengthens with mental exercise, like body muscles. Anybody can attain higher intelligence with the committed usage of the brain.

Studies show that people who learn to exercise their brain, perform better than those who believe they are gifted.

> "If, like those with the growth mindset, you believe you can develop yourself, then you're open to accurate information about your current abilities, even if it's unflattering. What's more, if you're oriented toward learning, with a growth mindset, you need accurate information about your current abilities in order to learn

> effectively"
> ~ Carol S. Dweck, Mindset: "The New Psychology of Success"

Dr Carol Dweck describes why many organizations, including Enron, failed, because they hired "talent" instead of people who learn and develop themselves continuously.[40]

Neuroscience indicates that parts of the religious brain atrophy when problems are left "In God's Hands".[41]

Religious organisations, like Christianity and Islam, install "Fixed Mindsets" that must remain rigid on pain of death and everlasting hell.

Intelligence of believers

Intelligence researcher Helmuth Nyborg showed in 2009 that <u>compared to Atheists</u> in the USA[42],
the average IQ was:

- 1.95 points lower for agnostics
- 3.82 points lower for liberal persuasions
- 5.89 points lower for dogmatic persuasions

---

[40] Carol Dweck: "Mindset:The Psychology of Success"

[41] Religious Experiences Shrink Part of the Brain – Andrew Newberg

[42] Nyborg, Helmuth "The intelligence–religiosity nexus: A representative study of white adolescent Americans". *Intelligence* 2009

Nyborg with others [43] also found that the world's most religion-based countries are consistently among the poorest.

Compassion

Laura R. Saslow with others found, in three separate studies[44], that religious people are less compassionate.

A mind that puts the love of God above all else, considers its fellow human beings secondary. This reduces compassion and promotes abuse by simply invoking the name of God, such as in the Dark Age, 9/11 2001 and many other incidents of terrorism, described "ad nauseum" in previous chapters.

Many witnesses of the 9/11 2001 events in the USA are still bewildered by attempts to understand how religious people can be so callous as to kill thousands of innocent people. Remember also that Adolf Hitler, Joseph Stalin and Pol Pot were educated in religion.

These atrocities confirm that compassion dies with religion.

---

[43] Lynn, Richard; John Harvey and Helmuth Nyborg (2009). "Average intelligence predicts atheism rates across 137 nations". *Intelligence*

[44] Laura R. Saslow, Robb Willer, Matthew Feinberg, Paul K. Piff, Katharine Clark, Dacher Keltner, and Sarina R. Saturn – "Compassion Predicts Generosity More Among Less Religious Individuals" – *Social Psychological and Personality Science* - 26 April 2012

Morality

The human species is a social animal, naturally co-operative and constantly developing ways to help fellow human beings. This promotes healthy personal ecologies. *This defines morality.*

Humans are also competitive, status-seeking, predatory animals. When these elements get out of control, personal ecologies become ill. *This defines immorality.*

The Role of Women

Women play a particularly important role in maintaining the moral health of society. Much less aggressive than men and more empathetic, women's perspectives on social conduct are better suited for establishing morally robust codes of behaviour.

Women already do this in important ways; by their choice of mate and how they establish rules in the home.

Whenever moral codes are considered, it must include a strong contingent of the fair gender.

Pushed to extremes of behaviour

Two personal ecosystems pressure competitive behaviour into extremes:

- **Too much power** leads to unchecked self-centred behaviour. This triggers predation and the impulse to enslave others. This ecology is adequately described in the chapter "The Lucifer Effect".
- **Too little power** results from desperate ways to satisfy one's needs. Trying to survive mentally and physically in harsh ecologies can lead to dysfunctional behaviour.

Criminal Behaviour

A vast majority of prison inmates suffered dysfunctional ecologies during their formative years.[45] A dysfunctional ecology entrains the brain into dysfunctional behaviour such as dissociation, alienated self; typical characteristics of prison inmates.

Ironically, prisons duplicate the dysfunctional ecology that created the criminal mind in the first place.

From an analysis of interviews with 65 incarcerated adults, Dr Abby Stein establishes the links between dissociation, distorted reasoning of the personal ecology, resulting from childhood abuse, and its impact

---

[45] Profile of Jail Inmates, 2002. U.S. Department of Justice

on adult violence. [46]

Religious Moral Code

Atrocities in the name of the religion are still ongoing. [47]

To test the assertion that religious people are more likely to adhere to moral codes, we examined immorality in terms of criminal acts. We compared the criminal inclination of religious people, with those free of religion.

We combined the findings of two independent surveys made in the USA, and calculated the probability of religious individuals adhering to criminal codes of society. We compared this to Religion-Frees.[48] [49]

The following surveys were used:

- The statistics of the ARIS (American Identification Religious Survey - 2009
- The 1997 Federal Bureau of Prisons Statistics report.

---

[46] Abby Stein - "Prologue to Violence"

[47] http://www.mindandreligion.com
[48] The statistics of the ARIS (American Identification Religious Survey - Barry A. Kosmin, Ph.D - Ariela Keysar, Ph.D) report of 2009

[49] The 1997 Federal Bureau of Prisons Statistics report.

The total population in the USA in 1997 was 266,490,000.

The following table shows the results using Religion-Frees as a base.

Group	Numbers	In Jail	% of Group	Criminality
Religion-Free	**29,481,000**	**156**	**0.0005**	**1**
Catholic	50,873,000	29,267	0.0575	109
Other Christians	108,641,000	26,162	0.0241	46
Jewish	2,831,000	1,325	0.0468	88
Muslim	1,104,000	5,435	0.4923	930
Scientologists	5,5000	190	0.3455	653
Total		**62,535**		

By comparing the **"% of Religion-Free"** group in jail (4th column) with the other **"% of Group"** in jail, we show the probability of a religious person having a **criminal record compared to Religion-Frees** is:

- 109 times more likely for **Catholics**
- 46 times more likely for **Other Christians**
- 88 times more likely for **Jewish**
- 930 times more likely for **Muslims**
- 653 times more likely for **Scientologists**

"I say quite deliberately that the Christian religion, as organized in its churches, has been and still is the principal enemy of moral progress in the world."
~ Bertrand Russel - "The Emotional Factor"

Rehabilitation of convicts

What effect do religious organisations have in encouraging morality in prison inmates?

Religious inmates in the USA constitute 98% of the total prison population. Studies show that over 70% of released inmates are re-arrested within three years[50]. Charles Manson, had spent most of his life in and out of prison by the time he instigated the murders of Sharon Tate and four others[51]. It appears that better interventions are needed.

The most effective solution found to date for rehabilitating convicts, is education. Care must be taken, however, to ensure that it is sanitised of political and religious indoctrination. Education increases self-esteem and empowers released prisoners with a boosted ability to re-integrate into society.[52] [53] Education is a nurturing

[50] Report of the Re-entry Policy Council: Charting the Safe and Successful Return of Prisoners to the Community
[51] Bugliosi, Vincent with Gentry, Curt. *Helter Skelter — The True Story of the Manson Murders 25th Anniversary Edition*, W.W. Norton & Company, 1994. ISBN 0-393-08700-X
[52] Steurer, S., L. Smith and A. Tracy. 2001. Three state recidivism study. Lanham, Md.: Correctional Education Association.

[53] U.N. special rapporteur on the right to education of persons in detention. 2009. United Nations General Assembly, 2 April.

process and supplements a critical psychological need for an abused life. This nurturing re-affirms personal value and willingness to take responsibility and ownership of self. To change the mindsets of inmates from takers to givers, teachers should be selected from the inmates.

We must re-assess the role of Religion in Society

Society without Religion

Robust Morality

Religious *misunderstanding* of human nature underlies much of the frustration caused by its ineffective morality.

An accurate and thorough understanding of the dynamics of personal ecologies is essential. Religious understanding of human nature is incomplete, distorted, and creates superstitious prejudice of Palaeolithic proportions. This sabotages the maintenance of healthy moral ecologies.

The Basis of Morality

What are the most effective paradigms that encourage moral behaviour? While the meta-physical paradigm focuses on the unseen, the pragmatic moral paradigms focus on down-to-earth personal ecology. Understanding the dynamics of personal ecosystems teaches us how to live in moral harmony.

A realistic understanding of self and others is vital for behaving authentically and therefore encourages a vibrant social circle. This is the key for developing a supportive ecology, which is the basis of moral behaviour.

The above may seem complicated. Luckily we have the brains for it. We only have to activate it!

"...if devotion to truth is the hallmark of morality, then

there is no greater, nobler, more heroic form of devotion than the act of a man who assumes the responsibility of thinking.... the alleged short-cut to knowledge, which is faith, is only a short-circuit destroying the mind. "

~Ayn Rand, Atlas Shrugged

Shrinking Believer Community

According to WIN-Gallup in 2012 [54], there has been a significant reduction in the percentage of believers in several countries shown here:

	2005	2012	%Change
Worldwide	77%	68%	-9
Vietnam	53%	30%	-23
Ireland	69%	47%	-22
Switzerland	71%	50%	-21
France	58%	37%	-21
South Africa	83%	64%	-19
Iceland	74%	57%	-17
United States	73%	60%	-13
Canada	58%	46%	-12

[54] WIN-Gallup International GLOBAL RELIGIOSITY AND ATHEISM – 2012 PRESS RELEASE

Waning church attendance

According to a Gallup Poll in 2004, in Scandinavian Countries, Germany and France, church attendance fell to *less than 10%,* in the United Kingdom and Northern Ireland, the Netherlands and Belgium attendance is *less than 15%,* and in Spain, Portugal and Greece church attendance is *less than 30%.*

In 2005 the number of people in the USA worshipping regularly is only 17.7% [55]

[55] *The Journal for the Scientific Study of Religion* - C. Kirk Hadaway and Penny Long Marler

Living Naturally

"There is something infantile in the presumption that somebody else has a responsibility to give your life meaning and point... The truly adult view, by contrast, is that our life is as meaningful, as full and as wonderful as we choose to make it."

~Richard Dawkins. - The God Delusion

Success is not dependant on religion. Humanity owes its success to evolution through natural processes. The more we learn to understand nature, the more we find it to be nurturing. Our senses are fine-tuned to harmonise, live, learn and grow within the ecology of nature. Thriving depends on understanding nature's processes.

Religion-Frees understand, live and nurture their natural capacities. Here are some examples.

Stride with Pride

The value of pride is noticeable in children such as toddlers, whose behaviour is not thus far filtered by beliefs. Parents are familiar with the excitement of their children when they learn something new, such as tying shoelaces or putting on their clothes for the first time. "Mommy, Daddy look what I can do!"

Pride is natural. Good parents encourage their children, with reciprocated excitement and pride, knowing the children are encouraged to learn and prosper.

An insidious submissive attitude is not the mindset of winners. It is unnatural and unhealthy. Successful people are constantly seeking to improve themselves for optimal effectiveness to reach their desired destination.

A submissive mind is vulnerable to predation by those who will commandeer it for their own purposes.

What! No Worry?

Hoping for intervention from the meta-physical world is no better than gambling with one's future. Religion-Frees face problems like anybody else; however, they find practical solutions.

Religious people wait for a sign from God. In the meantime, their inactive brain shrivels and becomes less proficient at finding neural pathways to solutions. Religion-Frees use their brains to analyse their *ecosystems* for solutions, often finding the solution in extended ecosystems.

Finding solutions by considering an extended ecosystem is the basis of the Einstein genius. Many scientists of his time were trying to understand why the speed of light is constant, irrespective of the source of the light moving toward or away from us. Einstein considered the problem in a wider and found the solution in the context of energy. The equation of energy ($E=mc^2$) puts the speed of light (c) with mass (m) as component elements of energy.

No Guilt?

Sometimes a positively intended action results in an unintended negative outcome. This creates a fear that the action will have an ongoing negative effect on the personal ecosystem. This stress we call guilt.

> "For centuries, the mystics of spirit had existed by running a protection racket - by making life on earth unbearable, then charging you for consolation and relief, by forbidding all the virtues that make existence possible, then riding on the shoulders of your guilt, by declaring production and joy to be sins, then collecting blackmail from the sinners"
> - Ayn Rand, For the New Intellectual

Guilt-Resolution Paradigm of Religion-Frees

- Religion-Frees recall their positive intention and re-affirm their altruism.
- Identify component elements of the ecosystems that affected the situation and find solutions.

Develop a Talent for Living

Problem-Solving is brain exercise. Religion-Frees do not wait for a sign from God[56] [57] but find the solution themselves. The brain develops continuously with use, ensuring ongoing success and a healthy personal ecology.

Learning from Others

Children learn by imitation and so do adults[58] [59]. If we focus on peoples' faulty behaviour, we unintentionally learn that observed faulty behaviour. Paying attention to the excellence in people stimulates the equivalent neurons in us and this makes us smarter. The person we focus on is inspired to continue developing their excellence. This is a great way to establish a healthy personal and social ecology! We learn from excellence.

---

[56] Rakic, P. (January 2002). "Neurogenesis in adult primate neocortex: an evaluation of the evidence". *Nature Reviews Neuroscience* **3**

[57] Pascual-Leone, A., Amedi, A., Fregni, F., & Merabet, L. B. (2005). The plastic human brain cortex. Annual Review of Neuroscience, 28

[58] On beyond mirror neurons: Internal representations subserving imitation and recognition of skilled object-related actions in humans - Laurel J. Buxbaum, Kathleen M. Kylea, Rukmini Menon

[59] Resonance Behaviour and Mirror Neurons – G. Rizzolatti, L. Fadiga, L. Fogassi, V. Gallese – Universita di Parma

Creating Destiny

Religion-Frees take full ownership and responsibility of self and know that the mind and body will in due course grow to fit the task. With growing mental and physical strength gained through focused activity, the reward of achievement is a vibrant, meaningful personal ecology.

Assess your skills; some require time and effort to learn. Study other people who have walked the path before you to learn how they acquired their skills. One can join specialised classes, but this does not replace the hard work of practice.

The famous, world-class golf champion, Gary Player once said "the harder I practice the luckier I get". Achievement fosters self-esteem. We know that brain and muscle grow with exercise and good nutrition. The route to achievement is through training, critical thinking and remaining competitive.

> "No matter who you are, no matter what you did, no matter where you've come from, you can always change and become a better version of yourself."
> — Madonna

Postscript

Two mischievous brothers were always getting into trouble. If there was a problem in the neighbourhood, suspicions usually fell on the two boys. The parents, at their wit's end, heard of a clergyman in town with a reputation for disciplining children. They sent the elder boy, the leader of the two, to this clergyman. When the boy sat down, the clergyman asked him sternly, "Where is God?"

The boy's eyes opened wide but said nothing. Encouraged by the response, the clergyman repeated the question in an even sterner tone, "Where is God!"

The boy's knuckles whitened as he grasped the chair, but did not answer. The clergyman stood up and looming over the boy, raising his finger he exclaimed once again.

"WHERE...IS...GOD!"

With that, the boy bolted from the room, ran home and into his bedroom. His brother followed, to find him cowering under the bed. He asked, "What happened?"

From under the bed his brother replied:

"We are in BIG trouble this time. God is missing and they think we did it!"

United by Nature,

We Are

Divided by our Beliefs

Appendix

The Brain

It is convenient to divide the brain into three main regions.

The Brain Stem joins the spinal cord with the upper brain and relays signals to and from the main motor and sensory systems to create movement of limbs and muscles. It is responsible for reflex actions such as the startle reflex, head/eye movement, breathing and heartbeat. It can be compared to the reptilian brain in both shape and function.

The Limbic System consists of a number of components that make us feel emotional about past, present and future experiences. The limbic system moves us to action. It regulates threat responses such as flight-or-fight, aggression, phobias and anxiety. It underlies our need for social contact, recognition, status and love. It is comparable to typical mammalian brains.

The Neocortex makes us human beings. It is responsible for understanding, creativity, imagination, fantasy and the expression of visual, physical and vocal arts. It is the daddy of invention. Like an umbrella it embraces the limbic and lower brain. It contains some 100 billion cells, each with 1,000 to 10,000 interconnections, and has roughly 100 000km of connections and growing. It is the thinking, conscious and, expressive mind, which processes large amounts of complex sets of data to extract the essence of being.

How important is the brain? We'd be dead without it.

Excessive Meditation and Depersonalisation

In a 1990 study, Richard J. Costello[60] records individuals who practice the type of meditation designed to alter their consciousness. It should be noted that some people may suffer depersonalization (loss of reality or a loss of identity) and derealisation during meditation.

Deikman (1963, 1966a) and Kennedy (1976) similarly reported cases in which depersonalization and derealisation occurred in individuals practising meditative techniques.

A study of six long-term meditators discloses that the acceptance of a 'depersonalized state of existence' is believed to be a sign of spiritual growth.

Deikman has referred to the effects of meditation as the de-automatization of the psychological structures that organize, limit, select, and interpret perceptual stimuli.

The danger is that a prolonged prayer/meditation altered state can become a permanent mode of functioning,

---

[60] Costello R.J. Psychiatry, Vol. 53, May 1990, pages 158-167 Depersonalisation and Meditation.

resulting in an inability to respond to important real-world survival issues.

The Allegory of the Cave

This allegory describes Socratic teaching of the concept of Forms, but is also interesting because of the dialog format in which it was taught. This format has come to be known as the Socratic teaching method. In essence it uses questions to engage the student. It is still used today by some teachers.

SOCRATES: Let me demonstrate how far our nature is enlightened or unenlightened:

Behold! Human beings living in an underground den, which has a mouth open towards the light and reaching all along the den; here they have been from their childhood, and have their legs and necks chained so that they cannot move, and can only see before them, being prevented by the chains from turning round their heads. Above and behind them a fire is blazing at a distance, and between the fire and the prisoners there is a raised way; and you will see, if you look, a low wall built along the way, like the screen which marionette players have in front of them, over which they show the puppets.

GLAUCON: I see.

SOCRATES: And do you see men passing along the wall carrying all sorts of vessels, and statues and figures of animals made of wood and stone and various materials, which appear over the wall? Some of them are talking, others silent.

GLAUCON: You have shown me a strange image, and they are strange prisoners.

SOCRATES: Like ourselves, and they see only their own shadows, or the shadows of one another, which the fire throws on the opposite wall of the cave?

GLAUCON: True, how could they see anything but the shadows if they were never allowed to move their heads? And of the objects which are being carried in like manner they would only see the shadows?

SOCRATES: Yes! And if they were able to converse with one another, would they not suppose that they were naming what was actually before them?

GLAUCON: Very true.

SOCRATES: And suppose further that the prison had an echo which came from the other side, would they not be sure to fancy when one of the passers-by spoke that the voice which they heard came from the passing shadow?

GLAUCON: No question, he replied.

SOCRATES: To them, I said, the truth would be literally nothing but the shadows of the images.

GLAUCON: That is certain.

SOCRATES: And now look again, and see what will naturally follow it' the prisoners are released and disabused of their error. At first, when any of them is liberated and compelled suddenly to stand up and turn his neck round and walk and look towards the light, he will suffer sharp pains; the glare will distress him, and he will be unable to see the realities of which in his former state he had seen the shadows; and then conceive someone saying to him, that what he saw before was an illusion, but that now, when he is approaching nearer to being and his eye is turned towards more real existence, he has a clearer vision, -what will be his reply? And you may further imagine that his instructor is pointing to the objects as they pass and requiring him to name them, - will he not be perplexed? Will he not fancy that the shadows which he formerly saw are truer than the objects which are now shown to him?

GLAUCON: Far truer.

SOCRATES: And if he is compelled to look straight at the light, will he not have a pain in his eyes which will make him turn away to take and take in the objects of vision which he can see, and which he will conceive to be in reality clearer than the things which are now being shown to him?

GLAUCON: True, he now

SOCRATES: And suppose once more, that he is reluctantly dragged up a steep and rugged ascent, and held fast until he's forced into the presence of the sun himself, is he not likely to be pained and irritated? When he approaches the light his eyes will be dazzled, and he will not be able to see anything at all of what are now called realities.

GLAUCON: Not all in a moment.

SOCRATES: He will require to grow accustomed to the sight of the upper world. And first he will see the shadows best, next the reflections of men and other objects in the water, and then the objects themselves; then he will gaze upon the light of the moon and the stars and the spangled heaven; and he will see the sky and the stars by night better than the sun or the light of the sun by day?

GLAUCON: Certainly.

SOCRATES: Last of he will be able to see the sun, and not mere reflections of him in the water, but he will see him in his own proper place, and not in another; and he will contemplate him as he is.

GLAUCON: Certainly.

SOCRATES: He will then proceed to argue that this is he who gives the season and the years, and is the guardian of all that is in the visible world, and in a certain way the cause of all things which he and his fellows have been accustomed to behold?

GLAUCON: Clearly, he would first see the sun and then reason about him.

SOCRATES: And when he remembered his old habitation, and the wisdom of the den and his fellow-prisoners, do you not suppose that he would felicitate himself on the change, and pity them?

The conversational, question and answer format of the above philosophical debate is call has become known as the Socratic Method and is still used by teachers today to engage students. It varies from the formal logic format developed by Aristotle.

The enduring interest....comes, I think, from the experiment's startling revelation of 'transformation of character' – of good people suddenly becoming perpetrators of evil as guards and prisoners becoming pathologically passive victims as prisoners in response to situational forces acting on them –(page 210)

In a situation where some people have the overwhelming balance of power and others are dehumanised and depersonalised, with no resources in defence, then abuse is bound to happen.

Major sins according to Islam

- Associating anything with Allah
- Murder
- Practising magic
- Not Praying
- Not paying Zakat
- Not fasting on a Day of Ramadan without excuse
- Not performing Hajj, while being able to do so
- Disrespect to parents
- Abandoning relatives
- Fornication and Adultery
- Homosexuality(sodomy)
- Interest(Riba)
- Wrongfully consuming the property of an orphan
- Lying about Allah and His Messenger
- Running away from the battlefield
- A leader's deceiving his people and being unjust to them
- Pride and arrogance
- Bearing false witness
- Drinking Khamr (wine)
- Gambling
- Slandering chaste women
- Stealing from the spoils of war
- Stealing
- Highway Robbery
- Taking false oath

- Oppression
- Illegal gain
- Consuming wealth acquired unlawfully
- Committing suicide
- Frequent lying
- Judging unjustly
- Giving and Accepting bribes
- Woman's imitating man and man's imitating woman
- Being cuckold
- Marrying a divorced woman in order to make her lawful for the husband
- Not protecting oneself from urine
- Showing-off
- Learning knowledge of the religion for the sake of this world and concealing that knowledge
- Betrayal of trust
- Recounting favours
- Denying Allah's Decree
- Listening (to) people's private conversations
- Carrying tales
- Cursing
- Breaking contracts
- Believing in fortune-tellers and astrologers
- A woman's bad conduct towards her husband
- Making statues and pictures
- Lamenting, wailing, tearing the clothing, and doing other things of this sort when an affliction befalls

- Treating others unjustly
- Overbearing conduct toward the wife, the servant, the weak, and animals
- Offending one's neighbour
- Offending and abusing Muslims
- Offending people and having an arrogant attitude toward them
- Trailing one's garment in pride
- Men's wearing silk and gold
- A slave's running away from his master
- Slaughtering an animal which has been dedicated to anyone other than Allah
- To knowingly ascribe one's paternity to a father other than one's own
- Arguing and disputing violently
- Withholding excess water
- Giving short weight or measure
- Feeling secure from Allah's Plan
- Offending Allah's righteous friends
- Not praying in congregation but praying alone without an excuse
- Persistently missing Friday Prayers without any excuse
- Usurping the rights of the heir through bequests
- Deceiving and plotting evil
- Spying for the enemy of the Muslims
- Cursing or insulting any of the Companions of Allah's Messenger

- Pride
- Allah has said in another place in the Quran:
- "And in this way Allah does put a seal on every arrogant disdainful heart." (40.35)
- 2. The wrath and punishment of Allah fall on the jealous person. Allah has said:
- "Certainly He does not love the proud ones." (16:23)
- It is narrated that Hazrat Moosa asked exalted Allah: "Oh my Lord! Who is the most deserving of your wrath and displeasure?" Allah Ta'aala told him:
  " It is he whose heart is filled with pride and his tongue is filthy (i.e. Abusive), his eyes are devoid of shame, his hands are miserly and he is of bad conduct and character.
- 3. Allah will put the proud to disgrace and ill-repute (dishonour) in the Hereafter.
- Hazrat Hatim Asam (rahmatullahi alaihi) has said: "Do not die in a state of pride, greed and arrogance."
- Allah does not cause the proud fellow to meet his death unless he is disgraced and dishonoured by his own family, relatives and servants.
- Similarly the greedy does not meet his death unless he becomes destitute for a morsel of food and a drop of water.
- In the same way the arrogant person does not meet his own death unless being polluted with

247

his own excrement and urine.

- 4. The proud renders himself liable to Hell in the Hereafter. It occurs in a Hadith Qudsi:

- "Pride is My cloak and grandeur is my trousers. If anyone disputes with Me in any one of these (two) I shall admit him into the Hell-fire."

- In the other words, pride and grandeur are two exclusive attributes of Allah, which none is allowed to apply and ascribe towards himself.

- It is imperative to refrain from such a dangerous and deadly calamity which leads to loss of knowledge of Allah, inability to understand the commands of Allah, His displeasure, disgrace in this world and the Hereafter and painful torment therein. No wise person can be neglectful in the matter of such a harmful and destructive calamity.

- We should, therefore, try to save ourselves from this and seek refuge from Allah.

- This is a brief account of the four calamities, mentioned in the beginning. Each of these four adversities are very harmful and dangerous in the sight of those wise and knowledgeable persons who are aware of the importance of the reforming of one's heart.

- Those are the four disease and vices that stem from having pride. How many of us are there that can honestly say, without deceiving ourselves that we are free of this hated ailment? Not many, is the answer. It is imperative that we take heed from this article and we bear in mind the punishment promised by Allah Ta'ala to those with pride in their hearts.

- Pride as a sin is incorrectly considered to be insignificant and minute in comparison to other major sins, by a vast majority of the people. It may be that compared to the major sins like murder and associating partner with Allah, it is slightly inferior. But that is only because of the magnitude of those particular sins that pride is considered a lesser sin.

- In a Hadith of the Holy Prophet it is narrated that, "Whosoever has in his heart, even an atom of pride he will not enter paradise."

- In observing the above Hadith, it is of utmost importance that we get rid of this spiritual malady, if we hold any illusion or hope of entering paradise.

Gospels

The historical accuracy of the Canonical Gospels has been questioned for a number of centuries. Here are some better-known researchers.

- The Jesus Seminar is a group of individuals, including scholars with advanced degrees in biblical and religious studies and related fields as well as published authors who are notable in the field of religion, founded in 1985 by the late Robert Funk and John Dominic Crossan under the auspices of the Westar Institute. The seminar's reconstruction of the historical Jesus portrays him as an itinerant Hellenistic Jewish sage who did not die as a substitute for sinners nor rise from the dead, but preached a "social gospel" in startling parables and aphorisms.
- Recent scholars, such as Dale Allison and Bart D. Ehrman continue skepticism of various parts of the New Testament
- David Friedrich Strauss (1808-1874) – a theologian and a pioneer in the historical investigation of Jesus, denied the divine nature of Jesus, asserting that the miracles of the gospels could be treated as myth.
- David Hume –*An Enquiry Concerning Human Understanding* - "Here then we are first to consider a book, presented to us by a barbarous and ignorant people, written in an

age when they were still more barbarous, and in all probability long after the facts which it relates, corroborated by no concurring testimony, and resembling those fabulous accounts, which every nation gives of its origin."

- Thomas Jefferson (1743–1826) - a president of the United States and the principal author of the Declaration of Independence, considered Jesus' ethics superb but the miracles not provable.

- Hermann Samuel Reimarus (1694-1768) – believed that human reason can derive the knowledge of God and ethics from a study of nature and internal reality; thus eliminating the need for religions.

- Albert Schweitzer (1875-1965) – viewed the Christian ethic as temporary. It was no longer relevant or valid and should be abandoned. In 1953 he won a Nobel peace prize for his "Reverence for Life" philosophy.

- William Wrede (1859-1906) - a German Professor of Lutheran theologian wrote on the Messianic Secret theme in the Gospel of Mark. He also wrote a crucial study, which argues against the authenticity of the Second Epistle to the Thessalonians (oldest Christian document).

- Rudolf Karl Bultmann (August 20, 1884 – July 30, 1976), a German professor of the New Testament at the University of Marburg for three decades. He defined an almost complete split between history and faith.